A Mere Rica

A Mere Rica

Linh Dinh

chax
2017

Chax Press / PO Box 162 / Victoria, TX 77902-0162

Chax Press is supported in part by the School of Arts & Sciences at the University of Houston-Victoria. We are located in the UHV Center for the Arts in downtown Victoria, Texas. We acknowledge the support of graduate and undergraduate student interns and assistants who contribute to the books we publish. In Sumer 2017 our interns are Julieta Woleslagle, Maria Edwards, and Renee Raven. The book is also supported by private donors. We are thankful to all of our contributors and members.

Please see http://chax.org/support/ for more information.

Cover photographs by the author.

Library of Congress Cataloging-in-Publication Data

Names: Dinh, Linh, 1963- author.
Title: A mere rica / Linh Dinh.
Description: Victoria, TX : Chax, 2017.
Identifiers: LCCN 2016052321 | ISBN 9781946104045
(softcover : acid-free paper)
Classification: LCC PS3554.I494 A6 2017 | DDC 811/.54--dc23

LC record available at https://lccn.loc.gov/2016052321

Why are you so mean, mommy?

Table of Contents

State of the Union

Shovel toothed, funky in profile,
I, John Dodo, am son of Camden.
Beneath boasting of a city invincible,
I'm two boarded up windows. I am a
Well-painted mural of kaput industries.
Who touches these, touches my void.

Once I shoveled coal, tamed pig iron,
Strung bridges. Erected. Now I strut
Up and down Broadway, dazed,
Fingering coins, aiming for chicken.

Pants low slung, crack peeping,
I'm son of Bethlehem. I peddle
Christmas mart, push Sands.
I patrol dying mall in Buffalo.

At dawn, in McArthur Park,
Los Angeles, I piss and scratch.
Legless, I buff Hollywood
Plaques, pose as monster
For tourists who undertip.

I push charity condoms, body oils,
High class looking purses, low class,
High definition porn, incense and sox.

Lying on news, ads and cardboard,
I browse, RECOVERY IS ON COURSE.
BUM SIGHTINGS DOWN. LATTE SALES UP.
BRITNEY SEEN IN ODD COLORED SHOES.
JUSTIN ALARMS FANS WITH FAKE HAIRCUT.

As I sleep, an asswipe sneaks
Photos, then gives me a buck.
Strung out, I will suck and fuck,
Excuse me, until I get my fix.

Like a cliché, I press nose
Against steak house glass.
Soon I will break that glass.

How to Have an Interesting Life

Shun the smart crowds. Instead, mix
With the dumbest you can find.
They will teach you much, in fact,
Just about everything. They'll show
You how inadequate you really are.

Sneer at beauty, especially all
Manifestations of glamour. Never
Forget that time brings each ugliness
And that we're all hideous, at the core.

(Coeur.) If you see unblemished skin,
Peel it. To nourish your atrophied
Sense of empathy, practice mercy
Fucking at each opportunity, and try

To do it sober. Don't, like every other,
Identify and align yourself with power.
Short of suicide, always situate yourself
In the wrong place, at the worst time. Be
Vulnerable. If you are "at home," you are

Not trying hard enough.

My Local Rising

You ask, “Must art be political?”
First of, art is always political.

Enter any modern art museum,
You’ll be greeted immediately
With Minimalist oils, the same
That decorate corporate lobbies, and
Unlike zigzags that gladden brutes, these
CEO-sponsored smears and stripes cost
Legs, nuts, torsos and even entire countries.
Huge yet hazy, they awe, but don’t irk clients.

Or take Abstract Expressionism.
Content-free, mostly, it appears
Apolitical, but it coincided exactly
With the hyper masculine posturing
Of the American state, or consider

Language Poetry. With its constant
Meandering and quick shifts, it
Echoes television, so that too
Is political, since it reinforces
The tranquilizing and flattening
Media tactics of our masters.

Pushing a glamorized death,
They want you to be divorced
From all that surround you,
Not just your city or town,
But the one you sleep with,
The food you eat, the room
You're in, this moment. Life

Is mediated, then. Between
One and all is a screen.
Fixated by this, I can't
Feel your breath on me.

Yes, I'm talking to you. You.
Frightening each other with
Our homely beauty, we must
Eat and have sex sideways,
But let's try, for good, to kiss
With no melody of any kind.
Canned tunes are our opiate.
Turn them off to hear ourselves.
Measure all with our bodies.

Eternal Flies and Postmodern Men

A fly alights on some feces, broods
On a dead man's face, then buzzes
Straight for the vermillion lips
Of a most radiant girl. For a second,
Her labial flesh is his cosmos. During
Its brief life, this fly has already had
A wider range of experiences than you,
And if it could talk, it would also be
Many volumes of books wiser than you.

Advanced, men fornicate high tech plastic.
A woman becomes moist reading texts sent
By a faceless, dickless Don Juan. Bothered,
She claws her infernal oven while typing.
Envying flies, he spills his fate on the floor.

Killed or Mauled?

Be grounded and raw, don't let
Life be filtered by any medium,
Be it an "educational" TV show,
Or a poem, especially this one, if
This is even one of those. Look

At this thrift store shirt, lavender
With cartoony figures, draped
On a lank body, at rest, during
A brief smoke break. Now hear,

Without looking, someone say,
"I don't know how anyone can
Get married, I don't know, before
They're 45. I mean, hello!" Then,

"I love that guy. I want to give that guy
My uterus." These specimens prove,
Once again, that a poem, any poem,
Is not so much written as found, so
Short of getting killed or mauled, go.

Away from this Mind Rape

When someone pipes, “I know Knoxville,”
What does he mean by that? I mean,
How much of Knoxville has he measured
With his own body? Once, I heard
A novelist declare, “Read my book
And you will know what Brooklyn was like,”

And I could only think, Her private Brooklyn
Can’t be larger than her medium-sized head,
So even a thousand-page book can’t do justice
To an inch of Brooklyn, which must be measured,
Directly, with your own two feet, and hands, too,
As you crawl or slither, or as you sniff Brooklyn’s
Infinity of sweatily fragrant spots. Thanks

To Fisher-Price, a newborn can now be strapped
To a seat, and forced, his head tilted up, to stare
At a relentless screen, with its bright and anxiety-ridden,
Sped-up world, so that his eyes will cloud over and roll
Away from this mind rape. Drooling, he will utter a series
Of terrified near-words, which his iPadded parents
Will interpret as pleasure. Raised in apptivity, kids
Will eschew walking, talking or eating while looking
At their food, or sex that isn’t on demand. Like now.
Hooked on porn and apps, we’re pacified.

Are you back yet? OK, then, walk with me.
Actually, don't walk with me, for our paces
And pauses shouldn't converge. Exiting
Girard Station, I notice a white-bearded man,
Leaning on a walker, saying, "Good afternoon,
Can you spare some money for lunch," while you,
Already down the block, stop at a table,
Set up by an old lady. She's selling old pots,
Five single rolls of toilet paper and an ashtray.
On a chain link fence, she has hung her dead
Husband's polyester jackets. A portable heater,
Well-rusted, is also for sale. You engage her.
Examining closely the ashtray, you can't help
But envy its coherence, focus and dignity.

Jerks

Revolution aborted by virtual sex,
Potential Paines stay home and jerk.

It's all good! Meanwhile, hiding at the U,
Professors lure the smooth-skinned and doe-eyed
Into always voting for what's disguised
As the lesser, sic, of two gross evils.

Between tenure, healthcare and undergraduate nookies
Or dissing Israel and the military banking complex, all
Will choose the quiche special in the faculty lounge.

"Fuck you, man, I invest in GE, Raytheon, Boeing, BP,
Blackwater, Halliburton, Titan, Bechtel and Aegis
Defense Services, because, fuck you, man, do you
Want me and mine to starve, working 9 to 9, like you?"

As daddies and mommies fund
Weapons of pax americana,
Sons and daughters occupy.

Intimacy

Leaving house or country, a man
May have skin contact with someone
His wife never suspects, may fling
His love or a hand grenade at those
He'll keep mostly buried under trash.

Late at night, though, he will relive
The nakedness of a lover or corpse,
As his bare foot touches his wife's.
He will feel estranged from this trusting
Flesh next to him, for it has never
Opened up to him like that other one.

The corpse, then, is his soulmate, since
It turned itself inside out just for him,
And to reciprocate, he unzipped.

To make his wife more urgent
And truer to life, more authentic,
He may have to invert her also.
Gun always cocked, he's turning.

7/4/13

Is it the Fourth of July yet?
So who should I shoot now?
Dude, can I jerk off your flag?
You're welcome to stroke mine,
Then we can both massage
The Constitution, you know,
Roll it up, like this, and stuff
It up the Liberty Bell's ass.
Man, I feel like voting again.
It's like eating bad Chinese.
Did you elect this emoticon?
I'm bored, let's waterboard
A whistleblower or two.
Global warming is cool,
So let's all sleep naked,
Just like Bradley Manning.
I've never heard of him either.
You know what kicks ass?
A flag tattoo on a corpse,
Or guys pissing on a corpse.
Let's snag some Army chicks
And make a naked pyramid.
Don't join if you don't want some.

Kill 'Em All

Sovereign countries are sandboxes
For Uncle Sam, as he loves to suck
The black stuff from beneath sand,
But don't blame me, I'm just another
Pissed off dipshit bored out of his wits
Among so much sand, so I wander
Off base to puncture some ragheads.

Male, female, old, young or just born
All look about the same, even alive.
Maybe I'll get on the cover of *Esquire*,
Like Lieutenant Calley, swarmed by gooks.

Biologically, we're programmed to love
What's most like us. I'm fond of my face,
And you don't have a choice but to adore
Your ape demeanor. It's how we're made.
Genocide, then, is built into the equation,
For each of you I kill, there will be more
Of me, proportionally, in this sick world.

What to make of my President, then,
For as a Kenyan Socialist Liberal Messiah
Who can hoop, slow jam and weep on cue,
When not cracking joke about drones, he
Resembles no American we've ever known?

Personally, I don't mind seeing that hue,
If it shuts up blacks and smart whites.
To keep oil gushing from bloody sand,
And steel boxes humming on asphalt,
They may even prop up a chick or spic.

Roaring, "Bye, bye, Miss American Pie,"
I'll strafe weddings, funerals and baby showers,
Blast children from their first English lessons.

Pigskin, Beauty, Death and a Huggable Rat

225 countries watch the Super Bowl, but
Almost none play. Unfamiliar with the rules,
They merely stare at a spectacle. Of all
American sports, football is one that hasn't
Spread overseas. It doesn't translate well.

The amount of equipment needed excludes
Poor countries, which are most of the world,
But its very nature also precludes
Global appeal. It is nonstop violence.
On each play, someone is knocked down,

But he doesn't writhe and grimace, as in soccer,
But gets right back up. With padded shoulders
And helmeted head, a football player appears
More than human. He is a machine. A robot.
A mascot for NFL broadcasts is a hulking,

Dancing robot. Thick necked and impervious
To pain, a football player is the opposite of
Your weepy-feely, pencil-necked intellectual.
The objective of each football play is to gain
Real estate. For tactical reasons, a soccer

Player often passes a ball backward, sometimes
Even to his own goalie, but in football, there is
Only the forward thrust. In fact, a backward pass
Is illegal. Gaining yards is so important, it defines
The success of each play, and of each player
Who touches the ball. A running back has

A successful day if he gains 100 yards, even
If he never scores and his team loses. In no
Other sport is statistics kept of yards gained.
A soccer or basketball player can dribble

The length of the court or field without tallying
Anything, but in American football, each yard
Must be counted. This nearly continent-sized
Nation has always defined itself by expanding,
By gaining yards and miles. Settle the coast,

Then foray inland. Move the indigenous
Out of the way. Kill them. Half of Mexico
Was swallowed up, then Puerto Rico,
Hawaii, Guam, the Philippines, on and on.
Now, America has at least 700 military bases
In 130 countries. That's lots of yards gained.

Granted, there are no people that haven't
Engaged in territorial wars with neighbors,
But the US's ceaseless reach is unmatched.
Much more than land, America invades minds.
There is scarcely a brain alive that's not

Constantly titillated and harassed by
American culture. Worldwide, people wear
Hats and shirts with American slogans
And words they don't understand. They listen
To American lyrics and babble American.

In Vietnam not too long ago, a woman asked if

I liked the song, "Aleet Beeper." What she meant
Was "Careless Whisper." Whatever its title and
Whatever it meant, she liked that song. Also
In Vietnam, I saw "POLO" stickered onto a

Japanese motorbike. This man had Americanized
His modest rice cooker, since America was much
more
Glamorous and cool than Japan or anywhere else.
Humans are warm, machines are cool. Notice
The ubiquity of "cool" to denote anything positive

In American English. Americans aspire to become
Hard, tough, and efficient machines that feel no
pain.
More specifically, they identify with their car, a
Sputtering box that enwraps them daily and gives
Them personality and status. Spending more

Time with his car than anything or anyone,
The American's confidante is his steel spouse.
Nowadays, it can even speak and tell him
To go to hell or the strip mall. Each year,
Car commercials dominate the Super Bowl.

Its main goal, then, is to push more wheels,
Oil, and by extension, wars for oil. Ignorant
Of draw plays and blitzes, even catatonic
Grannies in the Hindu Kush are compelled
To ogle the Super Bowl, since the empire

Exudes not just power, but a kind of sexiness.

The alpha male demands vigilant attention,
For he's cooly lethal. You can't duck him. By
His lizard-blooded calculations or whims,
Anyone anywhere may be blasted at

Any time by a plane or drone, even without
Knowing why. A study shows that only eight
Percent of Afghan men have even heard
Of the 9/11 attacks, America's pretext for
Maiming and killing Afghans. Even more

Than usual, war lurked behind this Super Bowl.
Before Christina Aguilera botched the Stars-
Spangled Banner, Lea Michele belted America
The Beautiful, so there were basically two
National anthems. Troops with flags arrayed

Behind these sirens. As Aguilera mumbled
And fluffed, we caught a glimpse of a grinning
George W. Bush. Our war-criminal-in-chief
Would appear again later, as would Condi Rice.
After Aguilera's last note, military jets roared

Overhead. During the game, we were suddenly
Introduced to Sergeant Giunta, a well-jangled
Veteran of our Afghanistan carnage. He stood
With other soldiers beyond the end zone, waving.
As has become customary, announcers thanked

All of "our troops" worldwide "for all that they do."
Earlier, there was a shot of American grunts
Enjoying the biggest game in Afghanistan.
America is gorgeous, but so is every other land.
None can match her in mass hypnosis, however.

In a 1997 article for the US Army War College,
Major Ralph Peters sums up America's cultural edge,
"Hollywood goes where Harvard never penetrated,
And the foreigner, unable to touch the reality
Of America, is touched by America's irresponsible

Fantasies of itself; he sees a devilishly enchanting,
Bluntly sexual, terrifying world from which he is
Excluded, a world of wealth he can judge only in
Terms of his own poverty." And, "The films most
Despised by the intellectual elite–those that feature

Extreme violence and to-the-victors-the-spoils sex–
Are our most popular cultural weapon, bought
Or bootlegged nearly everywhere. American
Action films, often in dreadful copies, are available
From the Upper Amazon to Mandalay. They are

Even more popular than our music, because they are
Easier to understand." The further one squats
From Uncle Sam, then, the sexier he becomes,
For without an actual experience of America,
This country is pure fantasy, a fabulous rumor.

One of history's oddest ironies is the name Mỹ Lai,
Which means "half-American" in Vietnamese.
Mỹ is "American." Lai is "of mixed race." If
A person is "Mỹ lai," he is half-American.
Mỹ in Vietnamese also means beautiful.

In daily Vietnamese, then, America
Is the beautiful country, Americans
Are the beautiful people, and the American
Economy is the beautiful economy, etc.
In the half-American village of a country

That calls America beautiful, American
Soldiers killed roughly 500 unarmed
Civilians on March 16th, 1968. Nearly
All were women, children or the elderly.
America seduces, then kills. During one

Of Israel's episodic massacres of Arabs,
I saw a photo of a dead child wrapped
In a Mickey Mouse blanket. Murdered by
An American bomb, she would be buried
With her beloved American icon. An American

Talking rat accompanied her to eternity. Watching
The Super Bowl, Americans and foreigners alike
Are blasted with this message: America is
Bombastically virile and stridently fun, if only
On television. The seats at this spectacle are

Way out of your reach, even if you dwell
Right here, in the cartoony belly of the beast,
But your seats at home are free, assuming
They haven't been pulverized by the USA.
Though you can never be this cockily

Carefree and invulnerable, this immortal,
You're free to stare, stare and stare...

War, Porn and Jive

Your bobbing head doesn't count.
To fudge ugly statistics, many
Of the jobless are depicted as
No longer wanting to work. Cute.

Voluntarily foregoing an income,
You're just not interested in eating,
Drinking or sleeping (under their
Sweating tonnage, granted, as they
Extract your last ounce), so say
A wet farewell to your shower head,
Flush toilet and one lemon-garage,
For you're hitting, hard, the potholes.

At fifty, you're starting over, son.
At twenty, you're done. It's never
Too late, or too early, to discover
The great outdoors, or to squat
In a trash, bottle, shit and needle
Strewn, post-industrial civilization.

Hey, do you parley Chinoise?
Fuck you! Fuck you! That's all
The Chinese you need to know.

Sun Tzu counsels, Feign disorganization,
Shape shift, make your enemy think
You're moronic, then one fine, sunny day,
As the still extant, mutant birds are chirping,
Blow up Goldman Sachs, JP Morgan Chase,
CNN, FOX, Times Inc. and the Disney Channel.

Yes, I can hear you loudly, bud, you'll cancel
Your cable subscription after the Super Bowl,
March Madness, NBA Playoffs, Stanley Cup,
Spring Training, then Opening Day, then, then.

Dearest Ministry of Propaganda, we're trying
To wean ourselves, sort of, from your manure,
But please, whatever you do, don't take away
Our free internet porn, OK? Snatch our rights
To breathe in peace, searching for cheap eats,
But don't mess with our right to ooze on
Our sofas, beds or bathroom floors, OK?

Only with porn, do we feel connected
To other people's inner or outer selves.
Transcending race and age, porn unites us.
Without porn, we'd just be narcissuses,
Each man, woman, child and dog with shard.
Without porn, we wouldn't know anyone, not

Unless we lived in a tent city, of course.
It's the first again. Are you making rent?
Is your phone still connected? What
About that gas bill? How many limbs
Do you have left? Did you serve them?

For butchering, did they toss you a slice
Of pepperoni and a made-in-China flag?
Will you waste someone soon? With them
Unreachable, will you zap yourself?

Sun Tzu raps, No nation can survive
Endless war and a deluge of bullshit,
So that's why you and yo mamacita
Are swirling up the Potomac, without.

Missed Connections

I noticed you behind the fat Chinese guy.
We have a history, I know, and I'm somewhat
Sorry about that. I'll send you six swift boats
To makeup. How about if we make love, again,
With my tonnage on top, again. I miss your pho.
[Uncle Sam to Miss Saigon]

Passing by, I couldn't help but see you being shoved
By the fat Chinese guy. Next time, call me and I'll
come,
Or maybe I won't, who knows, for I'm half owned by
That same obese asswipe who stopped buying your
Bananas over the Scarborough Shoal tussle.
[Uncle Sam to Luzon Palawan Mindanao]

Seeing you dumpster diving the other day, I meant
To say hello and toss you a quarter, but the Secret
Service wouldn't allow it. Plus, it would look phony,
For I did shove you out into the cold years ago.
Had to, or I wouldn't have made it this far, so
Just be glad for your old buddy, as you chew
Wet french fries and suck on leftover ice.
[Barack Obama to his soul]

Excuse me, my English no good, sucks ass,
But I see you all day long, every day, pleasing
Yourselves in the office, living room, bedroom,
Bathroom, with your pig pictures and videos,
And your tubs of pig, chicken and cow, and
I can't help but see you blown up from the sky,
By your machine, like I was, by your machine.
[A Yemeni drone victim to the American public]

Dead broke, you buy the commercials promising
An asskicking future, plus applause and gratitude
From your compatriots, but soon you'll be abused,
Humiliated then shot at, by your own even.
[The ghost of Pat Tillman to an Army recruit]

I know it's a long shot, but I've been trying
To look you in the eyes and speak slowly,
And listen to each of your inflections, amid
The cacophony of this madhouse where even
The tiniest man cannot help but bully and bluster,
Where crass power is the only currency, where
A sneering boy rides a dead man's cock
To add ghost inches to his petty fame.

Grays Ferry

The name itself is dismal. Stumbling
Into adulthood, I spent a year there,
On a narrow, much interrupted street.
My austere block had a single, sick tree.
Tim Fender and I rented a row house
For only 50 bucks a month. Basically,
It was a shell, bought by this gay man
Who thought he would fix it up, but
Grays Ferry made him so depressed,
He just had to bolt. Being Catholic Irish,
This hood couldn't have been congenial
To someone gay, unless he's a priest.
Still, I seriously doubt the neighbors did
Or said anything. They certainly didn't
Show hostility to Tim or me, two art fags.
Everyone suffered in Grays Ferry, and
In 1986, it literally stank, for there were two
Huge lots filled with garbage, thanks to a
Twenty-day strike by Philly's garbage men.

I had left art school without a degree,
For why borrow money to learn painting
From all these failed artists? Why not just
Slink somewhere and paint? Though I never
Amounted to crap as a painter, I've taught
Myself to write, sort of, instead of hocking
My life to a bank, just so I could be misled
And muddled by stunted or puffed up typists.

That year, I manned up and mainlined Celine's
Death on the Installment Plan and his *Journey*
To the End of the Night. After the first
Paragraph of *Death*, I knew there were risks
To reading further, but until I could finish all
One thousand-plus pages of these books, I
Didn't leave the house. It took me a week,
Then I started my own novel, from which
I'd read on UPenn's WXPN.
The response was great, actually, but
People were just astonished by my
On air delirium, for the writing
Was a goofy mess. I had to toss it.
(WXPN liked my raving so much,
It even made me a host, until I
Really went nuts on a live show.)

The Grays Ferry shell was freezing.
I ate badly, drank rather well, kissed
Rachel upside down, bit her lips, and
Not in a nice way, either. I apologized,
And I'm saying sorry again, for one
Can never say sorry enough. I'm sorry.
Any lived life will trail loose ends, but what
Are unforgivable are malice and betrayal.
For a month, Tim had a boyfriend then,
Much later, told me he wasn't really gay.
I wasn't too gay, myself, for my prospects
As human, artist and writer were pathetic.
Irrelevant, young artists and writers lie

On gray sheets and dream of greatness
As society sinks further into stupid.
Hi, I'm stupid. This is stupid.
Nice to meet you, stupid.

The local, though, can never be stupid,
But I didn't know it then, so I missed all
Of Grays Ferry's breadth and depth, which
I never bothered to investigate. Tense,
I talked to no locals. I simply assumed
My future was in New York or, at least,
Downtown Philadelphia. What a farce.
Had I mingled in Grays Ferry, I might have
Discovered its trade in soiled underwear.
For 17 years, neighborhood boys would run
To swank Rittenhouse Square, to sell their
Skid-marked Fruit of the Loom to Fast Eddie.
A UPenn drop out, Eddie also paid these
St. John Neumann kids to piss, shit or throw up
Into his mouth. He kept shit in pizza boxes.
Though HIV-positive, Ed had butt sex
With some of these teen-aged boys.
Before his trial, Uncle Ed died of AIDS.
Eddie studied economics, then music,
Married his high school sweetheart, divorced her.
The love of his life, though, was excreta.
Messy yet meticulous, he saved all of
His boys' underwear in 312 trash bags.

To be an artist, you must not blunt your
Troubling vision, no matter how queer.
Hedge and you'll be a half-assed punk.
To be true, you must be willing to die.
You must, as Gary Snyder says, "kiss
The ass of the devil and eat shit."
You must have as much integrity
As Uncle Eddie of Philadelphia.

Broke Poem

Another day, another bounced check,
Another ream of bills and applications.
Come, you can boost your joking income
By shoplifting, pole dancing or shooting, as
Our Prez greets our creditor, who's buying
This nation from nuked sea to corexit sea.

Is that a can of sardine down your pants?
Fridge empty, I have no more Monsanto
Main course or side dishes to go with this
Aspartame punch my brood is hooked on.
"Dad, why do I have two heads yet no brain?
Why can't I spell 'Bernanke' or 'crook'?"
Actually, I don't have kids, for I can barely
Appease bedbugs and banksters, as is.

"Pay your bill now or your phone will explode
In your brokeassed face. Cough up, or the FBI
Won't be able to eavesdrop on your palavers.
If you don't settle charges and penalties,
Plus interest, of course, Her Honorable
Janet Napolitano herself will crawl out of
Your plumbing, as you digest Reader's Digest."

I guess we ain't broke enough to reform
Into functioning poems, handcuffs or bombs.
As is, academic jive, voting and FaceBook.
Detonating endless violence, they preach
Symbolic whining to us hushed puppies.
Though broke, I'm no boneless chicken,
Fished from a dumpster, no way, for I
Will break my breaker with a shoulder
Mounted weapon of teflon destruction.

Strumming Broke

Tony pays $280 per month for a room
Merely two blocks from the cracked bell,
Now more dinged than ever, but only
To the eagle-eyed. 7th and Market
Is no free-fire zone, but street noises
Disrupt sleep all night long. Honks,
Sirens and drunken shouts jab into
His debt, bill and illness-filled dreams.

Tony often wakes with a headache.
With no kitchen, everything's nuked,
Or fried, surreptitiously, on a hot plate.
Soon he may burn everything down.
On each floor is a shared bathroom.
"One of these guys shits on the toilet seat,"
Tony sighs, resigned, sort of, to such shit.

Tony was born and raised in Kensington,
A traditionally Irish slum that's now
Irish, Puerto Rican, Black and Vietnamese.
Ever heard of a Kenzo Mouthwash? Look,
It's when you bite on the curb as someone
Like Rocky Balboa stomps on your head.
The last time I was there, a young woman
Had just been shot, and as I was snapping
Her large candle-and-teddy-bear shrine, her
Teenaged sis shouted at me, "Hey, you can't
Take photos! This is not a *show and tell.*"

Tony was delivering pizzas in Philly,
But that felt deadly, so he got a similar
Gig in Cape May, on the Jersey Shore.
On a good night, he'd earn 200 bucks,
Sometimes even more. Tony bought a
$40,000 home, then sold it
For a 20-grand profit. A dead uncle
Also left him 50,000. This was Tony's
Financial, social and philosophical peak.
What is your apex, buddy? Ah, don't say,
"The years before I was born," or, "The decades
After I croak." Say, "The moment they're nabbed."

(In drug rehab, Tony met Tina, whom I'd find
Dwelling in a Camden tent city. Freckled,
Redheaded and petite, she said she was
A former Miss New Jersey. She was cute.)

Though he has never heard of the word "busking,"
Tony has been busking for two years. He freaks
Strumming and singing in public so, this day,
He swills two cans of Pabst beforehand, outside,
Since he can't afford to get buzzed inside a bar.

"I'm too old to be arrested for public drinking. Plus,
I wouldn't be able to pay the fine." Diffident,
Tony stands in the back corridor of a nearly empty
Commuter rail station, in front of a Dollar Store.

"FROZEN FEATURE OF THE WEEK. $1."
With luck, he'll cover his beer investment,
Plus enough for reconstituted meat.

Brook is Broke

Working at Easy Pickin', Brooke had it made.
She could steal skirts, blouses, shoes and purses,
Though her many hair extensions, she had to buy
At other places. A girl has to diversify her aura
To keep the male gaze fresh. Evening, at the club,
She could pick and choose from all these beggars.
The next day, though, she might be too crap-faced
To drag her sweet ass to work, but it was worth it,
For we're not here long, and love mustn't be
dammed.
Inside her tiny, hot hovel, there's moisture on walls.

A firm, long-lasting man leaves a syrupy aftertaste,
Except most of them don't last more than a blink.
Markus, though, did hang around long enough
To leave her Caleb and Leesha, plus an abortion.
Of course, Brooke got some on the side, as did he,
Then he was sent away for a half-assed mugging.
Out after two years, Markus was ancient history.
Plus, he could no longer achieve wood. Serious.
Something weird must have happened in the clink.

Whatever, life moves on, including another abortion
Caused by one or another of Brooke's conquests.
The Indian doctor did say, though, "You might die
The next time. You already have four. I'm serious."

A week after the doc's blah blah, Brooke was back
On Delaware Avenue, in front of a Pina Colada,
Looking as hot as ever. By comparison, Rihanna
Ain't ish, not to mention that neon nightmare,
Nicki.

That night, all was back to normal, then normal, too,
The next morning, as she called her boss to say
That she was too under the weather to show up,
Except that, this time, he snapped, "Don't bother!"
"Are you serious?" But he had already hung up.

Suddenly broke, Brooke sold her food stamps,
Then her stolen bags, for next to nothing, really.
Last time I saw her, she already looked thinner,
And though she had always chewed gum before,
I noticed her lovely mouth was empty.

Broke Xmas Blues

You must know, these are the strangest
Of people. To them, a new day begins
In pitch dark, and a new year when it's
The coldest, instead of spring. They believe
In rebirth when things are most dismal, and
When the shit really hits the fan, their God
Will return to take them to another planet, where
There will be more petroleum and each day
Will be Black Friday, and the Walmart will be
Much bigger than here, on this puny earth, with
Its increasingly listless Christmas, which most
Now spell as Xmas, without any idea why.

Celebrating the birth of Jesus, half
Of them, at least, commit suicide by swallowing
Their tapped-out credit cards. Many also
Kill themselves after relentless self love,
For this is, without a doubt, the loneliest
Society ever. Most eat and sleep alone,
Even while married. Even on their weddings,
They feel absolutely abandoned, so
They sob silently while biting their lips, as
All the guests openly sob while clapping.
That night, bride and groom feast on a
Host of maxed-out credit and debit cards.

Lovely Mandy has an open marriage, so
Her husband is gone for months at a time,
Only to reappear suddenly, to save
On a motel room, while on his way
To the next love making target,
Which is no longer his lawful wife.
“Marriage is heavy,” I said to Mandy.
“It’s like embracing a corpse while crossing
This earth a hundred thousand times, or more,”
Maybe I didn’t say that. Don’t even know Mandy.

While war rages, with more wars to come, I cross
A near empty parking lot, towards a rock bottom
Liquor emporium, with its speaker blaring John,
Yoko and a bunch of kids now grown old, caroling,
“War is over, if you want it.” Not a chance, buddy, not
In this culture of endless war and desperate gluttony.

Next to a ratty tree, Santa is glum and has no color.
“This seasonal work sucks, dude,” he confides, “and
“They don’t even pay like in past years, but what the hell,
If I don’t take it, they can always hire another fat guy.”
For a fee, not payable in food stamps, parents can have
Photos of their offspring being cuddled by this suspect.
Pockets and souls empty, we stumble towards verdict.

Job Forum

"The objective is to remove
This surplus of humanity, that
Even if employed still aren't likely
To earn their daily allotment
Of degraded nutrients, but what
Is the most efficient way for us
To remove this mass that's clamoring
For scraps from the dismal end
Of the job market's digestive tract?"

"If you're making minimum wage, then
You're clearly a minimal person. Don't
Blame me for your deficient DNA and
Lifetime of ignorant decisions. After
Slacking off at work, you drive home
For five hours of Call of Duty shootfest
And free porn snippets on the internet."

"I have two friends who each worked three
Minimum wage jobs, just to survive. One died
After falling asleep at the wheel. The other
Nodded off while working at Wendy's. He dunked
Half of his right arm into the boiling oil
Of the french fry fryer. He's alive."

"Sure it can work. I'm a minimum wage
Salad decorator and sandwich sculptor,
And I can scrape by, fine, on what I make
Because I eat lightly, don't drink and have
Forsworn children, health care, car and house.
You just need to set your priorities straight.
I have a bachelor's degree, by the way."

Young American

Dad said he wanted me to move out
The day I turn 18, three months from now.
I live 30 miles from the nearest store.
Rural areas suck for many reasons.
I have no money, no car, and no friends
I can move in with. I'm desperate for a job,

So I've applied at Walmart, Ace Hardware,
Family Dollar, Dairy Queen, McDonald's,
Jack in the Box, Kentucky Fried Chicken,
Chick-Fil-A, Church's, Taco Bell, Subway,
Exxon, Sunoco, Citgo, BP, Hess,
Walgreens, CVS and Piggly Wiggly.
I figure someone will give me a chance.

If I do get a job, I'll still have to get there,
So I plan on riding my piece of crap bike
For however long it takes, and once there,
I'll towel myself off and even change shirt.
The cheapest efficiency apartment
Will eat up more than half of my salary,
But hopefully I can still get a used car
Before an SUV runs me over.

The Army would have been a life saver, but
I have obsessive compulsive disorder and
Attention deficit hyperactivity disorder. Since
I was seven, I've been drugged, so I do
Everything, like tying my shoes, slower.
That's why I can't be a soldier. Also,
I know a guy who returned from Iraq.
His face is messed up, and so is his brain.

At this point, I'm more than willing to move
Into the ghetto, though I've never been.
I do have black and Mexican friends.
I've also thought about getting me a tent
And sleep by the creek with all the weirdos.
It beats murdering my always nagging dad.
"When I was your age." Oh, shut the fuck up!

Plenty of people around here get by
On welfare, food stamps and the church pantry,
So there's no shame in that, but I'd really
Hate to start the rest of my life like that.

Backpack and Nut Indexes

Forget the DOW or Nasdaq, I give you
The backpack index. Meet Aslim, a
Purveyor of backpacks and purses
At Philly's half-dead mall, the Gallery.
It's back to school time, so backpacks
Should fly off the rack, but not this year,
Since everyone is broke, after years
Of sinking wages, or none at all, yet
The cost of anything has gone way up,
Including the price of nuts, which have
Been crossed from your grocery list, for
Who needs snacks, when there's not enough
Quarters and dimes left for regular meals?

Out of nuts, rice or beans, you can sell blood.
Out of blood, you can sell your lower half
For half an hour at a time, or else
Have it shredded overseas, under the flag.
Like a nutcase, you lunge forward, yelping,
"Better to kill 'em here, I guess, than there,
Though I hardly know which country I'm in.
Even home, I no longer know where I dwell.
Fighting for nuts, I'll leave my nuts right here."

Nutless, you will be deemed a hero, fool or freak,
As you roll down the street, with your small flag,
But at least you'll eat with what's left of your jaw,
Though you may have to loiter outside all day,
Behind sign, "HOMELESS VETERAN. PLEASE
HELP."
Nutless, you'll recall that hazy, sweet night
In your Chevy, after much Schlitz, when she
Rotated those dear dice in her winsome way.

Tri-State Mall Variations

It's 20 below, windy, and I'll surely croak
Unless I get a ride to the Tri-State Mall.
I'll kill you if you don't take me to this oasis
Of discount liquor, sneakers and payday loans.

Across from this sixth-rate temple to Capitalism,
An old man sells cemetery flowers. Buy roses
To place over your own grave, then say a prayer
For a life well-wasted inside the Tri-State Mall.

My entire youth was spent in this beauteous tomb.
I had my first kiss and sexual experience there.
I also got married, then divorced there. No doubt
I'll die in the Tri-State Mall in Claymont, Delaware.

For decades, people laughed, cried and gasped
Inside the Cinemagic Five, then they chuckled
When it was turned into the Comedy Lounge.
Actually, most of the movies were wretched, and
Most of those "comedians" should be sent to
The Howard R. Young Correctional Institute.

At 17, Marlene escaped South Carolina.
In Chester, she was the first to use dark eyeliners
And slash her jeans, showing some skin, but
What did those innovations get her? Nothing.
Now, past 50, she pours beer at McTullio's
On the lower tier of the dismal Tri-State Mall.

Chuck makes beef jerky out of sirloin steak,
Which he brings to McTullio's daily, to offer
Friends and strangers. His face radiates peace,
Thanks to his good heart and countless pints
Of Miller High Life, at only a buck fifty per.

Each day, an unemployed man comes and sits
Across from the rolling gate of a long-dead store.
Hey, is that a joke? Where's the joke? There's no
joke.

Actually, there is a joke. Today's headline: "More
Americans are rich than previously suspected."
Another: "Pope and Miley Cyrus vie for *Time*'s
Person of the Year honor. Repeat for Obama?"

Mariam's Baby

Just 19, Mariam peddles fancy
Pretzels at Philly's half-dead mall, The Gallery,
While her fiancé, Dominik, has a classier job,
Complete with health insurance, at Starbucks.
Domink's dream gig would be Whole Foods.

Even as she wears frumpy outfits, Dominik
Buys Mariam lots of brand name clothes, belts,
Purses and shoes, plus flowers. When jealous,
She'll smack Mariam good, though. Boiled over,
Mariam also claws herself bloody,
Screams and yanks her long, wavy, black hair.

After, her voice will be raspy, and for weeks,
Her face and neck will show these red marks. (Look
Closely, you can also see traces of a fixed cleft lip.)
It's not clear whence this coiled anger, despair
Or anxiety, for Mariam's life growing up wasn't
All that turbulent. Granted, the boys she dated
Were nasty enough, and sex sucked, so after
Enough grappling, she realized she didn't care
For any dick, whether micro or Holy Jesus.

Now she has Dominik. Soon, they'll get married
In New York State, where it's allowed, then save
Until they have six grand for some guy's sperm,
Preferably of the X kind, to be named Jewel.

By the time they have that kind of dough,
It might cost, Mariam jokes, a million bucks.
Sure it's odd to have an unknown's sticky cloud
Pumped into her, but this child will be sense itself,
And absolutely perfect, even after birth.

Work done, they walk hand in hand, but lately,
You can spot one without the other, and sometimes,
Dominik strolling with a brand new female, and
Mariam bantering with some security guy.

Boyish looking yet 40, he lives with his mom
But fancies himself a player. Looking at him,
Mariam beams her prettiest smile, even as
That familiar nastiness surges from below.

Beth

I never thought I'd see Beth again, but
She came bounding out of a dark doorway,
Called my name and gave me a hug. It took
A long while to figure out who she was,
For I'm awful at faces. Stories, I remember.
Plus, she has changed. It's been 20 years.

I first met Beth through a mutual friend, Phuoc,
That even he would mispronounce as Phuck,
As in Phuck Phan, kung fu master. In Vietnam,
Phuck was just a guy in dress shirt and slacks,
But in Philly, he grew his hair long and dressed
As if he was in a Hong Kong chopsocky.
You don't want to phuck with Phuck, though,
For he'd kick your ass. The many trophies
In his martial arts gym attest to this.
They were dating, but once, Beth came crying
Because Phuck was meditating and wouldn't
Touch her vagina. Pensive guys are already
Hit and miss propositions, much less dudes
Who meditate six hours a day, like Phuck.

Done with Phuck, Beth eventually married a
Japanese "sex champion," her phrase. They lived
In Philly for four years, then went to Tokyo
So he could die of cancer. There, his ex wife

Struck Beth with a rod several times when
They were alone. None of this sounded real,
Until Beth showed me a photo of herself
In a sauna with these Japanese broads.
This, as we were sitting in Dirty Frank's.

Today, though, we're in her new café,
And Beth was all wrapped up and flowery.
Staring hard at this Muslim hippie, I tried
To figure out who she was, then it hit me.
We'd kissed, but it was no big deal, except
Everything's indelible, to be retraced,
In due time, then blotted out again.
No memory is remote, only life itself.

Beth was talking about her third husband,
A doctor from Pakistan, "I believe
In commitments. With a commitment,
You can love anybody, but without it,
You can't love anyone. I tried it
And it was just emotional chaos."

Sunil at his Shopping Mall Kiosk

People who don't know South Asians think
We're all the same, more or less Indians,
But Pakistanis are Muslims, mostly,
While Indians are mostly Hindus and
Bangladeshis are much poorer than
Both Pakistanis and Indians. Although
A Bangladeshi, I was not poor at home.

Far from it. Back in Dhaka, I'd never, ever,
Eat lunch without meat, like today, with this
Ridiculous pretzel, with its smear of mustard.
Yesterday, though, Tumpa and I split
A Subway hoagie, on sale for five bucks.
Sometimes we also buy McDonald's, from
Their Dollar Menu, although it's not really
A buck anymore. This is bullshit, I'd think.
Why did I leave my decent life in Dhaka?

Back home, I would shop at Bashundhara City,
A mall ten times nicer than this Gallery bullshit.
This place is dying. It's, what, 3 o'clock already?
We've sold two necklaces all day. Imagine!
And customers also haggle with you now,
Just like in Bangladesh. When I first came,
Americans didn't haggle, didn't even know how.
Now they'll shoot off their mouths for 15 minutes
If they think it will save them a buck or a penny.

If this sucks so much, then why did I come?
But how was I supposed to know? Back home,
America appears as Paradise. You know, lots
Of money and everyone dancing and singing
All day long, and having sex, lots of wild sex!
Speaking of which, Tumpa and I barely do it.
You know, I never really loved her. In fact,
I don't even like her. I only married Tumpa
To come here. I mean, just look at Tumpa!

And it's not like we can even talk, because
She either makes no sense or she lies.
She lies to everybody. She'd tell people
We're about to travel to Niagara Falls,
The Grand Canyon or even Dubai, that
Last night we had dinner at Olive Garden.

All my girlfriends back home were gorgeous.
They didn't even look Bangladeshi, but Indian.
I know it's bad to talk like this, but it's the truth.
I wish I had never married Tumpa or come here,
But now, I can't return, for people back home
Would laugh at me for being a failure in America.

Yesterday, one of the security guards gave me
Two tickets for the flower show. "Your wife, Tumpa,
Will really like it!" He said. What a nice man, but
There's no way we're going, because I can't stand
To do anything with Tumpa. In fact, I can't stand
To even be seen with her in public. Oh wait,
Here comes Tumpa now, so goodbye, eh!
I'll talk to you some other time, buddy!

Not Getting Lucky in New Jersey

Jay Dee was with his woman for five years, saw her
Each day and slept with her every single night.
They had a great kid together. Only trouble was
She was bipolar, you know, so they'd argue, and
I mean screaming matches with things breaking.
Sick of it, Jay Dee decided, "We're splitting, but
I'm keeping Tim." Eyes bugging, she laughed, "You
Ain't keeping nothing, 'cause he ain't even yours."
Test proved it. Jay Dee wasn't Tim's dad after all.

Truth out, Jay Dee escaped to a go-go bar,
And blew, like, 700 bucks. He sat until closing,
And this chick, really hot, and blonde, too, said,
"Why are you blowing all your money?" He told her,
So her eyes went doggy sad, "I'm so, so sorry, but
You know what? Let's get a motel room. I'll make
Sure you feel a whole lot better." Here was this babe,
Nearly all skin, and glistening from all that dancing.
Her hand on his thigh, she rubbed against him.
Her breath smelled fresh, too. She was a baby.
There is nothing more infantile than sex. Though
Brandishing big words, we're nothing but babies.

What would you do? Not stupid, though, Jay Dee
Could tell she was only being friendly because she
Had seen his cash. He said, "I'm broke," and he was.
He must have spent over 300 bucks on her alone.
Sometimes he didn't even tuck bills into G-strings,

But threw money on the floor for chicks to pick up.
She murmured, “Don’t worry, I’ll pay. I just hate to
See you looking like that. I’ll do a good deed today!”
So they checked into a motel. It was only 53 bucks.

If I were fanciful, I could invent Jay Dee fiddling
The clock radio, to come up with Santana,
Nirvana or AC/DC, and on the wall, a print
Of Old Faithful or a unicorn, but since this is
Straight forward reporting, I can’t even claim
That her eyes were green, like a girl I used to know.
They drank Bud, did coke and he tried, you know,
To merge with her, but she said, “We need liquor.
Let’s go to your place and get us some liquor.”

She knew he had moved back in with his mom,
But the old lady was away, and wouldn’t be back
Until morning, so they went to his mom’s house
To get a couple of bottles. This was in Medford,
A really affluent town, you know, 97% white.
The English Manor is worth a million and a half,
With lots of trees all around, and spare rooms and
Bathrooms everywhere. He showed her around.
She was like, “Wow, you’re really loaded!” “No,
Only my mom is loaded!” He kept a close eye
On her this whole time, to make sure she didn’t
Filch anything. He didn’t blink for half an hour.

Never a book type, Jay Dee never went to college,
But he did learn how to do brick and cement works,
And even had his own business, with a truck and
two,
Sometimes three Mexican guys sweating for him.
Soon enough, he would also inherit a bundle, for
sure.

Back at the motel, they drank and he tried again
And again, but she kept stalling. I mean, he could
touch
But that was it. Then, she said, "I've got to call my
dad.
He's probably worried sick that I haven't gotten
home.
I'll be right back," and she went outside to call her
dad.
She was gone so long, Jay Dee started to think maybe
She won't return, and he'll be stuck with the bill,
But the door opened, finally, and there she was,
As hot as if she was upside down and red lit, but
Her disposition remained stale. They nibbled
Each other a bit, but only Jay Dee was naked.
Finally, she said, "Listen, it's not working out.
Let's just sleep," and they cuddled, which was nice,
Sort of, as he touched himself, until morning.
Parting, she gave him a phone number, but this
Was no more real than her name, Mercedes.
"Call me tonight, let's do something." They kissed.

From the top of the cul-de-sac, Jay Dee could spot
Half a dozen cop cars outside his mom's house.
Burglars had taken his mom's safe, with its 40
Thousand dollars, plus 80 more grand in jewelry.
There was no sign of a break in. They had entered
Through a back door left unlocked by Mercedes.
Jay Dee, then, became the only suspect, so
He was handcuffed right then, then locked up
For three months, until his case was thrown out.
Mom and son haven't chattered since, and Jay Dee
Has been homeless for eight months now. He sleeps
Outside nearly every night, since the shelters
Don't have enough sleeping spots, and assholes
Will cut in front even when you show up early, then
Rob you, so you must sleep with one eye open. With
Today's snow and sleet, buses have stopped running,
And people are falling left and right just trying to walk.

Check Fraud, Gas Theft and the Augmented Detainee Restraint

So now you know, don't take a stripper
To your mom's house, especially if
It's worth a million and a half, but
Jay Dee also has other lessons:

"Down to no money, you can bounce
Checks at different stores, and even
Get $50 cash back. At each, they will
Only scan your driver's license, and if
You haven't stiffed them before, you're fine.
Considering how many stores there are,
This can keep you going for a while. As
For your bank penalties, just make sure
You don't go over $500, total, or they will
Investigate you for check fraud, OK?

If you want to move to another state, or
Just drive around for the hell of it, you can
Get free gas. As long as you don't place
The nozzle in its slot after you've filled up,
They won't know the transaction is done.
By the time they realize something is wrong,
You've vanished. Also, it's best to steal gas
Just before you cross a state line. Cops
Won't likely pursue you in another state."

Jay Dee has also been a guinea pig, he claimed,
But the details are too weird. In Manhattan,
Someone shot something at his calf, then
Restrained him with electrocuting handcuffs.
There is such a device. Did the cops test
Their new toy on a homeless guy? Though a
Minor crook, Jay Dee broke no law that day,
Short of having no warm and soft place to lie.

James

Even if this economy was gravy,
James would still be in deep shit.
At 57, he sleeps in a trailer in a
Camden junk yard. In exchange
For this rusty haven, plus sporadic
Cash and food, he's the night watchman,
A slurry backup to the crazed bulldog.
The trailer has no water or electricity.
Each month, James gets 140 bucks
In welfare, plus 200 in food stamps,
Which he sells for $100 cash. Most
Of his meals are taken at soup kitchens.

Born in Camden, James has spent most
Of his life in Millville, NJ, the home of
Mike Trout, the 150-million-dollar slugger.
James has been to California and even Alaska,
But never out of the country. At 16, James
Fell in love with Linda, 14, and they had sex,
But they would not become husband and wife
Until 11 years later. They had twin girls, then
A girl and a boy, but the marriage

Didn't even last five years. A lifelong drunk,
James just drifted away, but each time
He showed up again, Linda would let him in,
Even after she had a new man. Sometimes
James wouldn't leave for two weeks. "I got along

Good with her boyfriend. I would introduce
Them to people as, 'This is my wife, and
This is her boyfriend.'" James spent decades

Working as a carpenter. He built houses.
Three years ago, Linda committed suicide
By swallowing a bottle of pills. James' children
All live near Scranton but won't talk to him.
He has never seen his seven grandkids.

Five years ago, James took vodka and crack
To this woman's house, "I was trying to
Score some pussy, you know, and we were
Partying over at her place, but I passed out.
When I came to, I noticed my wallet wasn't
In my pocket, but sitting on this counter. When
I opened it, my money was all gone! I had
Six hundred bucks, man, but it was all gone!

"She denied she had anything to do with it, so
I said, 'If you don't give me back my money, bitch!
I'm going to burn this place down!' She wouldn't,
So I went home and got a container of gasoline,
Returned and poured it on her trailer. I wasn't
Going to light it, I was just trying to scare her,
But she called 911. That's how I went to jail.
I plea bargained for five years and ended up
Serving four. I had never been homeless until
I got out of jail." While James was locked up,

His mother, a brother and Linda died,
But he didn't go to any of the funerals,
Since it'd have cost him 500 bucks
To be released each time, and he would have
To show up in handcuffs and shackles. "I didn't
Want to see my ma in a box anyway. My brother
Said she didn't even look like herself. She was
All bloated. I prefer to remember her sitting
At the kitchen table, reading her book.
That's how I still see her." This day,

James trekked across the Ben Franklin Bridge
To panhandle in Philadelphia, and that's how
I met him. James smiled, "Some people collect
Coins, others stamps. I collect jokes." He told me
Several unfunny jokes, including one about
A rueful Italian who's selling a blind horse.
His honest pitch, "He not looking so good."

I asked James if he had a photo of Linda,
And he said no, "It would make me cry
To look at her face." I said Linda means
"Pretty" in Spanish, and James said the only
Spanish he knew was, "Te quiero mucho!"

James has seven siblings, all brothers,
But three have died. A brother offered
To take him in if he'd sober up, but
James declined. This brother is also
Trying to quit alcohol. James has owned

Seven cars, but lost his last license due
To a DUI conviction. Female homeless
Drug addicts will offer sex for $20, even 10,
But fearing diseases, James is not tempted.

James doesn't have a woman now, "Because
I have nothing. I have nothing to offer a woman.
I take it one day at a time. At night,
I thank God for having given me a good day.
In the morning, I thank God for another day.
I thank him during the day too. I thank God."

Wall Wisdom

Since all prices are essentially cutthroat,
I steal or beg, which is also stealing.
Paying for a short ride, I cross country.
I forge checks, credit cards and barcodes,
Swap price tags, chat, eye and flirt
With the cashier to distract her. In love,
I also steal, beg and lubricate my
Grossness with measured ejaculations.
Paying for one life, I try to live several.

No Goldman Sachs, I'm just a nickel thief,
And like George Soros, I toss back a dime
After each sweaty killing. Leash led
By providence, I embody his plan.
I've been imprisoned, but that's
Because God wanted me to chill.
Sometimes it's good to go to jail.
Poking him, I accept his spanking.

Like a monastery, jail's a place to
Burp up and chew over your maker.
A man isn't man until he's cornered,
Thrashed then caged, preferably
On the most slanderous charges,
Just so he can grasp, finally, fate's
Funkiest form of mercy. It'd be good
To have this wall wisdom, though,
Without being enclosed by walls.

It's also good for a man to beg,
With his eyes bathetic and paws
Cupped together in supplication for
Something that will only come too late
To be more than a sick skit of desire.
Futility is the meaning of prayer.
After much praying, the fool wakes.
Locked together, like this, we rock,
Singly or in pairs, mostly singly,
Until we're let out, also singly.

Jackson in Camden

As a young man, I loved to fight.
Even sober, I'd fight. Though I'm not big,
I know how to throw a punch and mean it.
I never fought dirty, though. I don't like
These mixed martial arts queers on TV.
A man should always fight standing up,
Not on top of each other, on the ground
Sometimes, though, I'd get beaten, even
Knocked out. Three times I was arrested
And locked up for ten days, each time.
That was my only jail experience,
Before I got hooked on heroin.

I was born on a farm in West Deptford.
My dad and granddad were both farmers.
We even raised cattle, Black Angus, but
None of my family is in farming anymore.
I learnt cement work, and for thirty years,
I was a contractor. I had three trucks, a nice,
Three-bedroom house and five guys working.
There was so much work, I was running around
Like a headless chicken, putting out fires,
But after the housing crash, everything stopped.
I laid off my guys, sold my trucks then lost my home.
Looking back, I know I should have saved, but
Who knew it would turn out that way? Actually,
Irv Homer did. You know him? He was on radio.
In 2002, Irv started to talk about the housing crash,
And everyone thought he was crazy. He wasn't!
I used to listen to Irv and think, Shut the fuck up!

I've never been married, but my girlfriend, Jenn,
Was practically my wife. I treated her twins,
A boy and a girl, like my own children.
We went to the shore often, and I still talk
To her kids. I have another son, though. You see,
I've been with lots of women. Women like me.
I'm not like Wilt Chamberlain, with his 20,000,
But I've slept with, I don't know, over 300 women,
Ain't it funny, though, I've been with so many,
But I have no one now. I have a cousin
Who's afraid of pussies, yet he's married.
He's such a nice guy, it takes him an hour
To walk fifty yards down the street, because
Every three steps or so, he must stop and
Shoot the shit with one of this neighbors.

At 53, I may have blown my chance at love.
Plus, I have COPD, meaning I can barely
Breathe during sex. The last three times
I had sex, I couldn't make her orgasm.
I had to take a long break in the middle
To catch my friggin' breath, then afterwards,
It took me, like, God, forever to recover.
As you can imagine, she wasn't too happy.

Her name's Heather. She's a hairdresser.
We were together, off and on, for 12 years,
And I didn't cheat on her once! I was good.
Here, read this text, "I don't kno what u want....
Been waitin for u way to long!!!!....." She wanted
To get married, but I couldn't commit, so

Heather has a new man. Last Valentine's Day,
She gave me a card that could have been picked
By my grandmother! I had just gotten out of jail,
But I spent three hours in the Hallmark Store
To get her the perfect card. Now it's over.

I didn't try heroin until I was 49, and
Last year, I was clean from May 'till Christmas.
Now, I need three bags a day, one as a
Wake me up, one for fun, then one as a nightcap.
That's 30 bucks I must make each day, panhandling.
Food, I can get for free, and Medicaid pays
For my medicines. I take eight pills a day.
I'm not sure any of them works. I'm certified
As bipolar, paranoid and I have panic attacks,
But do you see how calm and lucid I am?
That's because of heroin. Heroin works.
Many days, though, I can't afford three bags,
So I must find used ones from the streets, but
You need at least 15 of these scrapies to get
Even a bit high, and once, I was locked up
Forty days for having six empty bags on me.

If you're arrested, they take $35 for the nurse fee,
But once I came in with 85 and left with nothing
Because the cops had stolen my other 50.
They had taken my glasses so I couldn't see
What I was signing when I was processed.
What's worse are the fines. If you're charged
With loitering in a drug zone, they fine you $500,
But all of Camden is a drug zone! They can also

Fine you for panhandling and obstructing traffic,
Then they'll charge you for the court cost too, so
You can easily owe them over a thousand from
A single arrest, and you're a homeless person!
The judge will put you on a payment plan
Of only $25 a month, but sooner or later
You'll miss a payment. That'll give them
Another reason to lock your ass up.

At least I haven't been killed out here.
One time a guy hit me with a steel pipe
Out of the blue. When I saw him coming
I thought he was just walking up to say hi.
I've been robbed several times, and a friend
Put a gun to my head because I couldn't pay
Money I owed him. I was thinking, Is this
How it's going to end? I wasn't scared,
I was just sad I hadn't spent more time
With my family. I'm talking about my kids,
And brothers and sisters, even the ones
Who don't like me very much. I said, "Al,
You don't need to do this. It's not worth it."
He took a deep breath and lowered his gun,
But then he said, "Put out your leg, Jackson.
I want to shoot you in the leg." "Fuck you!"
I said. "You're not shooting me in no leg!"
Al ended up not shooting me at all, and
I actually paid him back every single dime.
Three days later, I was walking on Linden
When I just started sobbing. I was so sad
I hadn't spent more time with my family.

At least I haven't died from an OD.
If you see an ambulance in Camden,
It's nearly always a heroin overdose,
Dealers do have a sense of humor, though.
Check out what they call heroin: Lights Out,
Dead On Arrival, Slave Master, Body Master,
Angry Bird, Death Row, Jersey Devil, Punisher.

Tim in Camden

I was born on Yom Kippur, the Jewish Christmas,
And my last name, Matusheski, means "God
Is with you," something like that. Look across
The street, and what do you see? Take your time.
You say "Crown Chicken, Angelo's Pizza and King
Gyro"? No, buddy, it says "Crown Angel King," and
That's no coincidence, because this city of Camden
Knew I was coming. Before this, I was in Skid Row,
In Los Angeles. You been there? No, it's no mess!
It may be aesthetically unsound, but not for long,
For the meek will inherit the earth, and that's why
I leave my vault of gold and my castles unclaimed.
I don't even know where they are. Doesn't matter!
I lack nothing. I've eaten today. I'm not hungry.
I'm really a Rothschild, but I've disowned them.
This morning, while shaving, I saw Jesus
In the mirror, and though He said nothing,
I understand a 15.0 earthquake is coming
That will swallow everything up, for this
Is utterly unacceptable! Prepare yourself.

The Happiest Place in Camden

Is not the aquarium, with its ménage à trois
Of sardines, tunas and anchovies, not even
Campbell Soup stadium, home of the Riversharks,
Though, it being winter, there are only steel dogs
All over the infield and out to shoo away seagulls,
No siree, the most ecstatic place in Camden, by far,
Is the McDonald's at the corner of Haddon and Federal.
First of, you'll be inside and not lying on the sidewalk,
And safe too, since the police station is across the street.
With trepidation and gratitude, I approach the counter
And beg, in my manliest voice, "May I have the transfat
Special please?"

"What's that?"

"With beef-flavored tubers too."

"You want me to call the manager?"

"I am your manager, baby. Can I have
The Black Anguish Extravaganza?"

"You mean Black Angus?"

"Whatever. Just give me that!
Give it to me. Give it! Now. Now!"

Floating on snowflakes, I glide into
My private booth, cradling my bubbly,
Flirtatious sweetie, my cor(o)n(ary) syrup
In its wax vessel. Like my Prez in his tank
Limousine, no bullet will pierce my tatters,
Long as I stay in this fortress. I tilt my head
To see my dad smiling down at me, for he,
Too, has lived in this city invincible, and has
Sat in this very booth in 1891, staring
At his own tray of meaty complications.

Camden to Trenton Train

In packed car, black man
With age-old shell game,
"Round and round she goes.
Where she is, nobody knows.
Bet twenty. If you guess right,
I'll give you a hundred bucks!"

Black or white, no old head
Would bite, for they'd seen
Enough hustling, and had,
Most likely, done a bit of
Pickpocketing themselves,
For who among you ain't
A shape shifting cheater?
On my right, a swindler.
On my left, an embezzler
And roof raising preacher.
Across from me, though,
There's a sexless saint, with
No gristle in his breath.

"Come on now, no one here
Wants a hundred bucks?
Just for fun, take a guess.
How about you, young lady?
Follow that dice carefully.
You're sure that's the one?
I'm going to open it. There!
You got it, but lucky me,
You didn't bet nothing!

This gentleman, though,
Wants to play for real. He's
A serious customer. He ain't
Got no time to waste now.

Round and round she goes.
Where she is, nobody knows.
Lordy, I'm getting nervous and
Damn it! He got me, so I pay up.
Here you go, Sir, a hundred bucks.
I'm a straight up dude. That hurts,
But if I lose, I lose. Let's do it again.

OK, young lady, you and your friend
Want to bet forty, to win two hundred?
You're going to clean out the house!
Lord have mercy. Round and round...
Don't get jumpy now. Look. Oops,
You guess wrong this time! Argh!
Who's next? Round and round she goes..."

Outside, the brief business strip
Of Palmyra, then booze-free Riverton,
Then Riverside, with its eight-story
Keystone Watchcase Company building.
None of these places are doing well,
But at least they're not Camden.

Out of $40, the young ladies
Brooded for a while. The white one
Had a baby in a stroller. The other
Was Puerto Rican, and chubbier. As
People grinned, she's getting more pissed
By the second, until finally, she got up
And charged the shell game man.

"I want my money back!
Give me my money back!"

"What you talkin' about?
We played. You lost."

"You cheated. Give me
My fuckin' money back!"

"Don't touch me, woman. If
You're gonna act like a man,
I'll treat you like a man!"

"I don't give a fuck. Give me
My money back, nigga!
I'm Camden, for real, so
Don't you fuck with me!"

"You touch me again, I'll
Seriously fuck with you.
Why don't you be a lady
And sit your pretty ass down."

Half a dozen men got up
To act as buffer between hustler
And this raging, tough talking fool,
So she kept going for a while, "You
Don't fuck with me, you faggot!
Bum ass nigga, you fuck with me,
I'll make you pay, nigga!"

Finally, she sat down, and after
A few minutes, the man came near.
"Had you been a lady, I might have
Given you something back, but no,

Not after all that, but this is what
I'm going to do. I'm giving $10 back
To your friend here, for her little man."
Addressing the white one, he added,
"And don't you share it with this bitch."

Using his life and brain as standards,
No man sees himself as a raw mark.
Fleeced, he chuckles at the others.
In sunshine, another fool is interred.

Dust Over Sheen

That night, I sat next to a large, elderly lady
Who snored quite prolifically. Even with a
Misaligned jaw and much fat gathering
Around throat, she managed to compose
Quite complicated, endless solos with her
Unconscious exhalations, but I probably
Did the same, so we must have been
Quite a duet, no less than Miles
And Coltrane during their primes.

Speeding through the dark, two tiers of strangers,
Past backs of homes, cars, car carcasses and
Radiant gas, burger and chicken oases.
With sun, we woke like old lovers, sexless,
That is, sans desire and with a touch
Of recrimination. I found out her name
Was Juanita. After working in government
For thirty years, she retired but now
Made money doing tax returns. "Incomes
Are definitely down," she said, "and some
Of my older clients are going back to work,
And we're not talking anything fancy, just
Retail and fast food, mostly. McDonald's.

Cost of living is going up, rent, gas, food,
But their social security isn't. You might think
It weird that they are competing against teens.
I mean, they can't possibly move as fast,

But having worked all their lives, they are
Definitely more responsible. I'm serious,
I'd hire a retiree over any teen.

Many kids these days don't know how to work,
And they don't know how to listen. You have
To write instructions down, because they don't
Know how to listen anymore. It's true.

Kids these days are too distracted. We all are.
From St Louis to Longview, Texas, there was
This young man behind me who was listening
To his iPod for about eight hours. I could hear
His music, it was so loud, and he was often
Singing along to it. How do you listen
To music for eight hours straight?

If there was loud music in the background,
Would we be able to talk like this? No!
No one can think, the economy is a mess,
And the weather has also gone mad.
Yesterday, I saw Pensacola
From the train window. It was like a bomb
Had gone off. And there's something else.
There's more dust in the air now.

There's definitely more dust in the air
Than when I was younger, but how
Can I notice it, if it's so gradual? But
I do notice it. I clean my house each day,

And when I wipe my TV screen with a cloth,
I can see more dust now. It's not soot, no,
It's not black, just dust. It must be because
We have fewer trees. I don't know how this
Affects human health, but it can't be good."

It can't be good, but it will have to be,
For there is no will to change anything,
Not when there's another tiresome tune
To jerk exhausted synapses, and more
Hyped narrations of pointless spectacles.
Though made from dust, our flesh balloons
As if pumped by endless gas, until gassed.
Outside the train, endless parking and cars.

Odd Beings on Sidewalks

Until yesterday, I hadn't run into Dan
In a few years, so was surprised
To see his hair still black, his body
Still muscled, with only the slightest
Hint of a beer belly. "I was never much
Into drinking. I smoke weed after work."

"Still, man, you look great! Look at me!"

"You know, I'm half Asian."

"Well, I'm 100% Asian,
And I look like shit."

Dan said his mom had just died, so
He had to hustle home to make a pot
Of chili to bring to his dad in Fogelsville.
His brother, Cyrus, was in jail again,
For, what else, dealing drugs. Dan
Used to be his brother's partner until
He got an office job 25 years ago. Once

When he was really trashed, he told me
About killing some black guy with Cyrus,
But I never got to the bottom of it. Now,
Dan's a good dad and husband, with two
Nice houses, one in Sea Isle, New Jersey.

White hair runs in my family. We're all born
With white hair sprouting from our hearts,
And though we appear so ancient tumbling
From that tunnel, we stay immature
Until we're laid out in that final box.

A shutterbug, Dan shoots pedestrians as he
Rides his bike to and from work, or as he walks
His shih tzu. "People are very odd animals."
With bodies coming in waves, causing awe
And arousal, we raise machines to our faces.

Freakish being, come here. No less odd, I touch
Your head like I'm your dad, but I'm not your dad,
Since you're my mom, but I don't quite know that,
So in my confusion, I kiss your forehead, then
Your closed eyelids. Since we don't know how
To do anything according to nature or nurture,
We lie perfectly still until the eyes are away.

I Talked to a Man

Who thought he might be Superman. He had a S drawn
On a piece of paper attached to his knit cap. "If you have
Blue eyes, you're set. With blue eyes, you're invincible."

He was black.

I saw an old woman putting pebbles in her purse
And throwing them, repeatedly, down the grates.
I noticed on two magazines, "MICHAEL JACKSON–
FOREVER THE KING OF POP" and "ANGELS
AND MIRACLES–THE SPIRITUAL REALM
AND THE WORLD YOU KNOW." Then I was asked:

"How often do you beat your dick?"
"Say what?!"
"How often do you beat your dick?"
"Why are you asking me that?!"
"I just want to know. You masturbate?
How often do you beat your dick?"

Chuckling, I walked away, but turned back,
"All the time!" which brought a relieved smile
To the face of this black teenager, maybe 17.
I didn't shake his hand. He did seem frail.

Ah, the wonder of English, which allowed
A tenth generation slave descendant and a first
Generation geopolitical refugee, both collaterals
Of the Yankee fantasy, to communicate perfectly
And spontaneously on the street. Through a brief

Spill of blurted gutturals, we confirmed our common
Jerkhood, but not all's well, because I went home and
Read that 26 Asian students had been beaten up
That same day at South Philadelphia High.

"Any girl?" my wife asked when I told her.

Our basest instinct is to look out only
For our own kind, I suppose, but let's not
Go there no matter how bad this thing gets.

English lesson: try not to say "thing." What
The hell is "thing"?! Vallejo did say "thing thing,"
However, meaning the penis. Speaking of dicks,
My midget is eternally on the cusp of pronouncing
His first word. Though he's extremely stupid and can't
Get past A in the alphabet, I've never beaten him.

Rabbit's in Grinnell, Iowa

"You know what I never get tired of?
Looking at beautiful American women!"

"Yeah, I've had my share of the slanty eyes.
In Vietnam, you had to stick a carrot up into them,
To make sure there wasn't a razor inside."

"My boyfriend just got back from Iraq. Either that
Or Afghanistan. I always get those two confused."

"We used to pick up drugs in California,
Sell it in Ohio and other places. Once,
Me and my boys were jumped by a bunch
Of Mexicans, but we retreated, called backup
Then taught them not to mess with Hells Angels.
This happened at a McDonald's in San Ysidro.
I've only been in jail twice. Once, I tried to shoot
This motherfucker in the head, but got his thigh,
And that's what I told the judge, too. 'I wish I had
Hit his head!' The judge gave me five years. I got
Out after four for good behavior. It was enough.
The second time was after a night of drinking
At the Rabbit's. I was so fucked up, I just drove
My truck to the police station, two blocks away,
And asked them to arrest me. The cop, good man,
Let me sleep in a cell until morning. He didn't even
Lock the door. It's just like a hotel. You should try it."

Freshly arrived, I shouldn't try to test
Much of anything, but then again, I could,
Since I'd be gone before consequences.
Here, there was no echo at any corner.

The carrot sticking man wiggled off his stool,
Then hobbled out of the bar on two crutches.
His right pant leg was empty below the knee.
Though born there, I'm fully here, unlike him.
I'm not haunted by bloody carrots and worse, though
What harass me through the years leave him alone.

I consulted the barflies on the local economy, bad,
And the pros and cons of turkey gizzards, good,
So I ordered what looked like a huge testicle,
And ate it with knife and fork, like fine dining.
It was a humbling and brave salvage operation.
Bathed in Tabasco, even the worst is palatable,
But this chewy and gamey knob was actually good.
I poured the American woman beer from my pitcher.

Tom Fischer's Tavern

Even blind, you can tell
What kind of a bar you're in
By listening to the canned tunes.

Sinatra's "Summer Wind,"
Cash's "Ring of Fire,"
The Band's "Up on Cripple Creek,"
Chicago's "25 or 6 to 4,"
Croce's "Time in a Bottle,"
Then, most unexpectedly,
Arlo Guthrie's "Alice's Restaurant,"
Which I've never heard in any tavern.

Arlo's rambling confuses the barkeep,
An Italian-looking woman, maybe 32,
"What the hell is this?" "Arlo Guthrie,"
I pipe up. " It's Woody Guthrie's son,"
But she has never heard of Woody, so
I try, "Do you listen to Bob Dylan?"
No, she says, so that's that, but at least
Now you know where you are, a trough
For middle-aged white guys. It's afternoon
And we're in Westmont, New Jersey.

Some bars are black and white, but more
Are almost exclusively black or white, and
Seldom will you see an Asian guy, like me,
Save in California or Hawaii. In Philly's

Chinatown, there is no neighborhood bar.
In beer commercials, though, everyone
Drinks, laughs, flirts and celebrates together.

Here, they've been talking about food,
As in fried chicken, pig's feet, beans and rice,
And grandma's killer egg and potato salad,
But now the chatter turns to water parks,
So a 55-ish gent tells the smiling barkeep,
"I can sit on one of those tubes all day long.
It's most relaxing, and you don't have to get
Out of the water unless you have to poop."
"To do what?" She asks, looking alarmed.
"To poop. Ahhh, it is relaxing to soak
Your butts and privates in that water.
It's only, like, four feet deep, you know,
So if you're fat, like me, your bottom scrapes
The bottom, as you glide along, in that water."

Shaving hell, we too will frolic until
We turn to some bottom material.
Like sediment or memory, we'll blur
To our true shape, leaving nothing,
Not even an icky smell, in Westmont.
Outside, flags everywhere and a sergeant
Named Rambo, I kid you not. Here, I'm safe
And whisky comforted. That's fair enough.

Allentown Bar

From Monday to Thursday, Freddie's
Is open at 8AM, so those on their last legs
Can swill cheap sud for breakfast, soon after
They've frowned at their wrinkles in the mirror.
Everyone gets sloshed here, blacks, whites and
Puerto Ricans, and even a stray Vietmanese
On this blustery day. The young white cook has
A black boyfriend, and the white, middle-aged
Bartender has a stolid black girlfriend.

Working class people are often bunched together,
And more often than not, they get along. Redneck
Wise man and wise guy philosopher, the awesome
Joe Bageant said something like, "Each White Trash
Family I know has black relatives." Some choice
Overheard tidbits from the hoppy congregation:

"Hey, how come every fuckin'
Weather chick is pregnant?
Every fuckin' one of them!
Horny bitches."

"Today's forecast, fifty percent
Chance of pregnancy."

"To get pregnant, you have to come
Together. If you come, like, in two
Fuckin' minutes, and she comes in ten,
It ain't gonna happen. You have to
Come together."

"Ladies, you must get your man drunk
If you want him to last a while, but then
You'll turn him a fuckin' alcoholic, not
That he ain't already."

"Speaking of the weather. I don't
Give a shit about the weather 'cause
I live just down the street, and I work
All day in this heated shithole."

"Ten more years before I retire, but
I don't want to think too far ahead. Shit,
I might die tomorrow, know what I mean?"

"Yeah, buddy, I just get up each morning
And try to hustle a few fuckin' bucks,
That's all. It's all I can do."

When the news came on about Romney
And Obama doing lunch at the White House,
Behind closed doors, the bartender said,

"Yeah, they probably
Have some fuckin'
Hookers in there!"

"It's all right. You're just a bullshitter.
It's not your fault, buddy. You fucked
Up my entire world. It's all good."

Friendly Lounge Sampler

"Take these Mexicans, they live
Ten to a house. Some of them
Only have one bathroom to share,
So what do they do? They must piss
In the sink or outside, and there's
Only so much hot water, you know,
In the morning, so someone must take
A cold shower, or fuck, no shower before
Going to work, and they do work hard."

"Check this out. Yesterday I was stopped
At the corner of 4th and Arch, and there was
This Chinese girl, maybe 14. It's hard to tell
With them, you know, no offense, and she was
Crossing the street, while talking on the phone,
But she had a set of keys and some money
In her hand, like this, and this black chick
Just knocked it out of her hand, and as
The Chinese girl bent down to pick it up,
The black chick just stepped on her hand,
Then took the money and ran! There were
All these people there, and I was in my van,
So I leaned out and shouted, 'Yo! Yo! Yo!
What the fuck are you doing?' And you know
What the black chick said? 'Shut up, white boy,
Finders keepers!' The Chinese girl looked like
She was about to cry, but now she knows. Never
Show your money, not in this city. Finders keepers!"

"I drank all night, took some Xanax this morning,
And I'm drinking again. Fuck, I must be nervous.
I've got a date tomorrow, and I'm already fucked."

"Yeah, man, I'm beat, nervous and fuckin' stressed.
I met with my new landlord this morning. I just hope
He won't look at my credit too closely. I hope
He won't call my last fuckin' landlord. I hope
We can move into this house. I've got two kids,
You know, and this is a safe neighborhood."

"Did you know coal came from outer space?
I heard it in the news, APR, but everything
Is already carbon anyway. That's all we are.
We came from coal, that's right, and we'll become
Coal, again, after we're dead. It's like recycling."

Same Old News

After decades of good, bad or middling,
Probably mostly bad, yet touching,
Heterosexual sex, middle-aged farts
Can let their inner homo flare up,
As in this Friendly Lounge exchange,

"You fucked me good there, buddy.
You shouldn't have done that." "Hey,
Take it easy, man. I did use Vaseline."
"No, you didn't, not this time, you didn't."

More often, the bonhomie is straight
Forward piggish, as when the Lebanese
Weathercaster appears. "I bet her poop
Smells just like curry!" "Ah, that's nasty!"

"I'm into lots of weird shit, but I'm not
Into poop. I'm sorry! I'm just not." "Hey,
I'll give her a good smell test. Hummm,
You're right, it does smell like curry."

Then tick local, national and international
Murders and rapes, targeted or random,
Nearly all done by tailed humans, of course,
Then Oscar Pistorius, that double amputee
Olympics runner who just shot his girlfriend
Four times, through a bathroom door. "What
A waste of good pussy! How can you get mad
At something like that? She's too good looking."

Scanning this dim dive, you'll see
A sad sack bunch of well-pickled
Priapic corpses not yet interred.
With pricks, they've erected skyticklers,
Defended motherlands against their kind
And bored their way across this globe.

"I think I'm about done. I'm fucked up!"
"That's what you said yesterday." "Hey,
I'm sorry to be a drunk." "Hey, I'm also
A stinking lush, but I'm no alcoholic!"

Suddenly a live female walks in,
Changing the room's static and even
Brightening each poor boy's outlook.
Each cadaver's tongue felt fresher.
Behave, children, for your teacher,
Whatever her name is, is here.

Ed's Sex Life

Shellacked, Edward fell asleep waiting
For a hypothetical bus. As he dreamt,
Someone played with his foot, but
It was no giggling lover, as he thought.
She or he nudged harder, so Ed smiled.
"Wake up! What are you doing here?!"
Opening his eyes, Ed saw a cop, took
A moment to figure out where he was,
Then got up to trudge home in the snow.
His feet were cold and wet. Someone
Had stolen his $80 pair of sneakers.

Ah, but how can a man go through a day
Without ten thousand mishaps, at least?
And we're not counting the insults even!
Each tick above ground is mushroom gravy.
You've crossed the line, though, if you asked Ed
About his missing arm, out of the blue.
There's no graceful preface or segue.

"When people say something stupid
About my missing arm, I tell them
I got an infection after fist fucking
Your mom. You got that?" Ed smiles.
"People would extend their left hand,
Or wave at me with their left hand."

Once, Ed had so many limbs, he ignored
Most of them, so a bunch felt sad, atrophied
Then fell off, but Ed didn't care, he had so many
Arms and legs left to toy with. Didn't we all?

Maria's Cures

Maria believes in invasive solutions.
If you have hemorrhoids, for example,
You can shove an aloe vera leaf
Up your ass, "But you must make sure
You peel the spikes off. If something's
Wrong with your vagina, an aloe vera leaf
Can also be shoved into your vagina."

As for penal punishment, Maria
Believes that Christina Regusters,
A woman who raped a 5-year-old girl,
Should be impaled by a red hot poker.
"I'll shove it into her myself, and I'll
Make sure it's flaming hot! I believe
In law and order. You ever heard of
Rafael Trujillo? He was a dictator.
He'd chop your fingers off, pull
Your finger nails out. I like that!
I hate criminals. I like law and order."

Maria also told me to abstain from eggs,
Cantaloupe and papaya after sundown.
She brightened when I said I liked mangu.
Though Dominican, she wore a jade bracelet
And had a reddish buddha on her keychain.

Ecco L'Americano!

Remember All in the Family strip club?
Don ran the pizza parlor across the street.
Don employed his hot girlfriend. She stole.
Don's handsome but dull. His dad arrived
From Abruzzo at age 53. "As a kid,
I was called wop, dago, grease ball.
You just ignore it. What can you do?"

Don's been back to Italy 25 times.
His family home is still there, but
The orchard with its olive trees and
Grape vines has been sold. Also, "Locals,
Not gypsies, have broken in to steal just
About everything. Each time they see me,
They shout, 'Ecco l'americano!' They ask
All kinds of questions about this country.
I love Italy, but I love America more.
Everything is better here. Everything."

Today, Don is morose, "It hurts to lose
Twenty thousand dollars. It happened
In Atlantic City. They stole my debit card.
I was sleeping in the Taj Mahal. It hurts."

Don's oblique confession needs filling in.
Sounds like he lost downstairs, then was robbed
Upstairs by a prostitute. Perhaps she did sound
And smell like a normal girlfriend while it lasted.

Sunlight glazes Don’s shaved jaw and Bud Lite.
We’re the only two drinkers in Friendly Lounge.
Football season and early darkness are coming.
People are killed, nations wrecked, porn comforts.
“If you lose your parents, you lose everything.
I have nothing, no home, no wife, no nothing.”

Poking Around South Philly

Half a century ago, South Philly
Was mostly Italian, but also Irish.
These groups linger, but now
South Philly also has many Asians
From China, Vietnam, Cambodia
And Indonesia. In the last decade,
Mexicans have also appeared.
Blacks live west of Broad Street.

In the window of a Chinese bodega,
There is a male potency ad, "HARD
TEN DAYS. A GRAIN OF SOON
THE EFFECT REVELS ALL NIGHT.
HOLD OUT FOR LONG TIME
TO POSTPONE ENLARGE
A CAPSULE. SUN SOURCE
LIVING CREATURE. WORLD
SEX ASSOCIATION." Reading that,
I wish I was a much harder poet, but
It's too late to change my limp habits.
I can't even type well, much less revel
For ten "long time" days. Do call 911.

Immigrants will infuse or infect
Host neighborhoods with charming
Or annoying habits. On 7th Street,
A Cambodian sells barbecued pork
And chicken on the sidewalk. Eaters
Sit on little plastic chairs. I inhale
The smoked meat aroma. Next time.

A block away, five flags transform
A brick porch into a small fort, manned
By a middle-aged white guy, sipping
His can of Bud. Another house has
One large flag and five small ones.
Erected for Memorial Day, these flags
Will stay up until the Fourth of July,
And into the nuclear winter, perhaps.
Hard from the dawn's first gleaming,
Through the bombs bursting in air.
Revel through the perilous mayhem.

Bombed, many came here. Shot at,
We'll fight back or leave, but where to?
And who are we, exactly? At Anna
Marie's Café, we are whoever will pay.
Blacks, whites, Latinos and Asians
All march in the door, shouting, "One,"
"Two" or "a sixer," and the barkeep
Will remember if it's Coors or Colt-45.
Only here is a beer named for a gun.
Giving $1.50 in change, she says,
"Here's a hundred and fifty, honey.
Spend it wisely." "I'll try," he laughs.

Marlon Brando, Al Pacino, Frank Sinatra
And Marilyn Monroe are all over the walls,
But Elvis and James Dean also lurk. Behind
The bar, there's a sign, "Confucius Say
Bad tipper Get BAD next drink." Notice
How "s" has been chopped from the verbs,
As a joke, of course, but let's be honest: In

This brain-scrambled time, we're all handicapped
With ghastly grammar, a wee vocabulary and
Decomposed spelling, so that "too" is routinely
Confused with "to," "it's" with "its," and "who's"
with "whose."
Confusion say sucky speaker get sucked dry,
And not in a hard ten day, reveling sense either.

Hardly anyone makes sense. Poets are fogged up,
But who cares about them? No one reads poets.
Let's listen, then, to Vincenzo, a regular,
Extraordinary guy, "I was born in 1945.
I have known my wife since I was 13,
And she 11. In 1965, we married.
For our 50th wedding anniversary,
We might go to Italy. We've never been.
My father was born in Latina. At 24,
He came to this country, then returned
Eight years later to marry my mother.
They would never see Italy again.

This neighborhood has changed so much.
When I was young, all the Italian mothers
Would scrub the front steps once a day.
Not once a week, but once a day, because
Everybody else was doing it. Each Friday,
We would eat Chinese. There was but one
Chinese restaurant in the neighborhood.
I would have pepper steak or pork lo mein.

Most of my life, I have done cement work
Or work at gas stations. I had a boss
Who said to me, 'Don't steal. If you need
Something, just ask me.' A great guy, he died
When he was 45, over five bucks' worth of gas!
A man had filled up but didn't want to pay.
My boss reached for his steering wheel.
He died when this asshole drove away."

At 50, I have owned a car for less than 2 years,
So I can't drive away from anything, including
The next war over gas. Stiffed, we'll die in place,
For there's no escape from this gassed globe.
Meanwhile, beer, pork lo mein and naked words...

T-Barr's Bar

On two televisions: Phillies and monster trucks.
On a shelf behind bar: Pluto the Disney dog,
Taoist scholar Lu Tung-pin, a unicorn and
Other kitschy figurines. On the wall: a guitar
With "Jack Daniel's" painted on soundboard,
Gift shop print of two Mexican peasants,
The Twin Towers, "Legal Capicity 40 People,"
Marlon Brando as the Godfather and famous
Photo of sailor kissing girl in Times Square
On Victory Over Japan Day. They didn't even
Know each other, and he was just grabbing
And kissing every female, young and old.

We're on the edge of Little Cambodia, but
There are no Cambodian pubs near, just as
There are no Chinese taverns in Chinatown.
"Do Cambodians come in here?" I asked Jimmy,
The bartender. "Yeah, sometimes, but usually,
Just for takeouts, and since it's Sunday, they're
Down by the lake, having their barbecues."
(That would be Meadow Lake, by the
Out-of-commission Navy ship yard.)

On my right, an old black guy would shout
"Strike," "Ball" or a phone number off the TV.
He jokes with himself, "He said it's just off
The plate, but I don't see no plate! Do you?"
Suddenly, he sings Meatloaf, "I want you,
I need you, but there ain't no way I'm

Ever gonna love you, but don't feel bad."
Then, "Baby, we can dance all night!"
When a middle-aged black woman
Comes in, he yells, "Hi, baby girl!
How are things?" "Things are things.
Bills, bills and more bills, but what
Are you gonna do? Things are things."
"Bye, big girl," he says as she leaves.
Another minute, and she may outgrow
Her shoes and clothes. "Every pretty lil' girl!"

On my left, a tattoo-coated white guy says
To Jimmy, "I've been drinking since three.
I couldn't sleep. I got up early."
To his left, a young black guy gulps,
In silence, glasses of Hennessy. He's
An oddity in a joint that deals mostly
In Bud, Coors, Hurricane and Colt-45.
When he steps out, Jimmy turns to me,
"I can't stand that guy! He's so ignorant,
But they're all like that. I can't stand them!"
The old black gent has also left. Soon, though,
The Hennessy dude returns and starts to bitch
About what happened to him last night.

"Me and this homie was at the titty bar,
And he must have robbed me, man, 'cause
I woke up and my money was gone, and
I know I didn't spend all that. I had
At least 7,000 by the time I left.
Fuck this motherfucker, I'm gonna

Blow his fuckin' head off. I'm gonna
Give him one chance to make right.
You fuck with me, I'll blow your head off!"

After Hennessy leaves again, Jim says,
"Now, who talks like that? You don't say
You're going to blow someone's head off,
'Cause you don't know who's in here. There
Might be a cop sitting in here," as in me,
Jim probably half suspects, "and he didn't
Have 7,000 either. He's just blowing hot air.
I know he's a drug dealer, but still, he didn't
Have 7,000 on him, but they're all ignorant,
Like I said. They talk all kinds of bullshit but
They don't care about nothing. They don't care
For their parents or even each other. They're
Just ignorant, that's all. I can't stand them!"

The Phillies will go on to lose another, while
Monster trucks careen and flip, delighting
A mostly white crowd. They have names
Like War Wagon, War Wizard, Grave Digger,
Brute Force, Martial Law, White Knight, Havoc,
Toxic, Americrush and Blown Income.
Drivers also have nicknames. There's Medusa,
Who's also known as The Queen of Carnage.

A small man sits with his can of Steel Reserve.
He confesses he is Luis, but not how long
He's been here. Judging from his English,
He got here a while back. Rising at 5:30,

Luis travels each day to Allentown for work
At a gardening center. Luis pots plants.
At his previous job, in a candy factory,
Luis had a Vietnamese manager, so
He has learnt, "Đụ má mày, làm biếng!"
["Fuck your mother, you lazy bum!"] When
Your boss or manager jokes, you better laugh.

Forty-five-years old, Luis has two grown kids
Who won't talk to him, because he couldn't
Provide for them. He has a lady friend
Who calls him "Pappi," but for variety,
He also meshes with Guatemalan and
Mexican whores, for they're reasonable.
"Thirty dollars! I don't lie. Thirty dollars!"
"Man, that's cheaper than Chinatown!"
"Fuck Chinatown! It's 150 in Chinatown!"
"They do wash your balls in Chinatown, though."
"I can wash my own balls! If you want,
I can take you right now. Thirty dollars!"

Everyone knows Mexican prostitution
Is in Philly. Hell, there's a Mexican whore house
Two doors from me. I didn't know it was so cheap.
Also, I've seen no cholo yet, but soon
Enough, they will come, guns ablaze.
Luis agrees. "The cholos don't play, man."

Buzzed, I leave with "Chinga a tu madre"
To Luis, who yells back, "Đụ má mày! Làm biếng!"
I ask Jim, "What time you open in the morning?"
"Ten O' clock, my friend, but for you, 9:55!"
Cheap bar, true people, I give T-Barr's five stars.

Deadly United States of Underwear

Scraggly bearded dude had an upturned
Finger etched onto the back of his neck,
But he didn't seem like a fuck you type.
In jean shorts, a mustachioed paesano
Rubbed his Yuengling belly with both hands
As he kvetched to his pal, "Yours is bulging
Sideways, but mine is shooting straight out.
I'm going to have a boy, and you a girl!"

Among four men and a woman, the barkeep,
There wasn't a single button, for all
Were wearing a T-shirt or muscle-T.
Freefalling superpower, we've become
The United States of Underwear. In
A few years, maybe, no American
Will know how to tie his shoes. On TV,

Our brain cell flushing is already frightfully
In high definition. Question on Who Wants
To Be a Millionaire, "What is commonly
Placed over the opening of a Corona?"
First of, who cares?! Still, among the dangled
Answers, the ditzy contestant could choose
A) Taco Bell Chalupa (product placement)
Or C) Sombrero, I kid you not, and though
The correct burp was clearly a wedge of lime,
She sweated along with host and audience.

Peeling from T-Barr's Bar, I drifted home
Through snug gauntlets of row houses. Though
Not much can grow here, there's a Tree Street,
And even a Mountain Street. This kind of
Flash magic is also deployed on countless
Majestic murals dotting dismal hoods.

At a pre-school, Discovery Place, I espied
A banner congratulating Mo'ne Davis,
"Scholar & Athlete." Sagging attire
Mirrors droopy thinking and writing,
So a 7th grader is now a PhD,
And this banana nuclear power and
Tireless sower of chaos is, even now,
Stridently trumpeted as mankind's succor.

As I type, our prez is pushing war, again.
From plumber to college president, we're
Passive killers, at best, so as our bombs
Tear through other people's flesh, we'll see
And say what we're told to see and say.

Meeting Uncle Sam at Samy's

While it's true that a hangover prefigures death,
So does a host of other events, missing a bus,
Stealing a kiss, sniffing something gross while eating...
Still, I've had enough of Miller High Life, that headache
In a bottle or pint glass, too many of which I swilled
That evening at Samy's, while chatting with Uncle Sam.

A short guy acting huge, Sam had been in the US
All of five months. Coming from China, he had landed
Somewhere in California, though his accent was so thick,
I couldn't make out which city he had stayed in. After a month
In that sunshine, he ended up in overcast Philadelphia.
"Sam," he blurted, "that's my name. I'm Uncle Sam!"
Coming to where America was born, Sam will get
To see her commit a mass murder and suicide finale,
Though by then, he might have to flee back to Guangzhou.

OK, so Uncle Sam had no job yet, and no skill set
Beyond a willingness to schmooze, for he had become
A regular in this black bar. Having bought a 99-cent
Bag of chemical-dusted potato chips, Sam shoved it at
A chick who had just walked in. Pissed, she shoved such
Right back. "Hey, hey, you remember me!" Sam shouted.
Playing peace maker, I grinningly said, "Punch him!"

With little English, Sam spoke in clichés, slogans and
Commercial pitches, "It's all good. Just do it. I'm lovin' it!
It's better here." In short, Sam conveyed nothing but
His own giddiness, but in that, he's no more silly than
The real Uncle Sam who preaches to us daily that
Happy days are here again, life's looking up,
The recovery is picking up speed, we will be
Energy-independent soon, there's a resurgence
Of American manufacturing and Detroit is back, etc.

Stripped of production and pride, we must swallow,
As if we're already brainless zombies, an endless
Buffet of hollowed out phrases: Winning the future.
We're the change we've been looking for. Change
We can believe in. Betting on America. Yes we can!
Meanwhile, America continues to hemorrhage,
With the latest, the announcement that chickens
Will be shipped to China to be slaughtered, then
Shipped right back here, to feed all the fired
American workers, pinching their food stamps.
Hunched in shelters, cars or tents, a million plus
Homeless American school children will munch
On killed-in-China, chicken-like poo poo platters
Once a month, when the welfare check arrives.

But don't sweat, Sam sings. Just listen to the kids.
"Ma, I want to grow up to be a drone operator!"
"Me, I'll get a PhD, then work as a pro snuggler,
Charging a peanut butter sandwich an hour!"

"I'll volunteer at the same soup kitchen I eat at!"
"I'll sign up for a badass uniform so I can explode
From a mine in a country I've never heard of." Good
As any, these are the plans as we blunder forward
Towards that mass murder and suicide spectacle.
With his flesh chopped up, Sam will eat himself.

Kensington's Best Bartender

I've worked at R, One and a Half and now, here,
Bentley's Place. The other bars are closed.
There are no customers left. They've all been killed.
Just this week, a guy was hacked with a machete
Across the street. Two weeks ago, two guys were shot.

It's the drugs, you know. They do it right in here,
In the bathroom. I've caught a few. The men's room
Has no lock, but the ladies' room does. Some girl
Would go and stay in there like, you know, forever.
I'd knock. She'd scream, "I'm doing a number two!"
Bullshit you are. I'd pry open that door with a knife
I keep behind bar. Sometimes they'd get so scared,
They'd drop that needle right in the toilet! Blood
Would be seeping from their arm. They'd be pissed
Because they didn't get their high. Whatever.
A guy would come in, order a beer, then nod off,
And I'd have to kick him out, too. He'd say,
"I didn't get enough sleep last night." Bullshit!

If you show me an attitude, you're outta here, but
I don't have to like you to serve you. I can't stand
Lesbians, for example, but I still serve them.
I saw these two lesbians on TV kissing each other.
They were, like, 89-years-old, and they were going
Muah, muah, muah! Yuck! Actually, I don't care
If they were 20. It'd still be gross. If I want to

Fall in love with a woman, I can just look
At myself in the mirror. Like my ma said,
"There's a lot of sausages out there," and
She should know, she had 21 children.

I came here when I was only one-month-old, but
I've been back to Puerto Rico three times, when
I was eight, fourteen and twenty-one, when my son
Was only two-years-old. He's thirty-four now,
And still living in Kensington. My daughter also.
I raised them right. They know right from wrong.

For fifteen years, though, I was an alcoholic.
I'd go through two fifths of Southern Comfort a day,
At least, plus other stuff. I'd do five drinks at a time,
All different kinds, rum, beer, wine, Southern Comfort,
Plus a cocktail. Whatever. Customers would buy me
Drinks up and down the bar. Once, though, I fell
Backward and was knocked out cold. An ambulance
Had to come, but at the hospital, I jumped right out
Of that ambulance, and somehow ended up back here.

Yeah, I know, it was only three blocks away, but still,
I was way gone, you know. The ambulance had to
Come pick me up again. It wasn't my last time.
I'd go four days without eating anything but
A slice of bread, just to soak up that alcohol.
My hands would get all gnarly, like this, so
I couldn't open my fingers, so I'd have to go

Into the hospital for the IV drips. Finally,
A doctor said, "If you keep going like this,
You'll never see your grandchildren, so what
Do you want more, your grandkids or booze?"
That's when I finally stopped, and I haven't had
A single drop of alcohol in 15 years and a half.

They said I was a trip, but I was flying
Without any luggage, so I had to change.
Though I'm around alcohol all day, I don't crave it.
This Christmas, I'm making two batches of coquito,
To make extra cash. It's a Puerto Rican eggnog.
It only costs me 6 bucks a bottle, but I sell it for 18,
And I'll probably sell 30 bottles, at least, this year.

I see new faces all the time, but sometimes, I'd jump
When a guy shows up. Hey, wasn't he shot? Did he
Climb out of the grave just for happy hour?
Like they say, it's hard to leave Kenzo. Even
When you're dead, you still need to return.

Sunday Afternoon at Jack's

"Are you Chinese or Vietnamese?" She asked.
"Vietnamese," I said. "I know some Vietnamese,"
She continued. "Boo coo dinky dow. You know
What I just said?" "I actually don't," I answered.
"I don't think it's Vietnamese." "Of course it is,"
She retorted. "Boo coo dinky dow! It means
You're crazy!" OK, so it took me a while
To figure out that she meant, "Beaucoup
Dien cai dau," which is a mishmash of French
And Vietnamese for "Lots of madness."
During the Vietnam War, this was often said
By locals to American GIs, and vice versa.

Across from the old lady was a man too old
To have fought in "Iraqi Freedom," though his cap
Brightly proclaimed him as a veteran of that
Open-ended campaign for petroleum and Israel.
Iraq has been broken for good, with the resultant
Chaos necessitating America's meddling
Until she herself collapses, which can happen
At any moment, even during the halftime of this
Much discussed game, to be followed by another
Endlessly debated spectacle. "Hey, can I take
A photo of you and your cap?" "I don't care,"
The old man replied to my request, "you can
Take a photo of my balls if you want to!"

His first war was Vietnam, his last Desert Storm,
And he has managed to survive it all as a cook.
Though his white beard has seen so much, none
Of it will be transcribed properly. Meanwhile
Utter nonsense is endlessly pumped into
Our much befouled national brainpan.
Our lives in arrears, we're expected to be
Transfixed by Rich Kids of Beverly Hill.

In a peaceful country, to leisurely get drunk
With your neighbors would certainly qualify
As happiness, but in a nation that can't stop
Mass murdering, even as its cupboards wheeze,
Each laugh is tainted with anxiety and blood.
As our cash is sucked upward, everything
At street level has gotten shorter, even the
Name of a Chinese takeout, Perial Palace.
Death murals and shrines mark drug corners.
It has become extravagant to be left alone
With a cheap pint, as the juke box whines.

Suddenly the bar roared, and I knew the end
Had come early to New England, for they were
Already behind 23-3. Here, no one cared really.
It was just something to watch on television.
Plus, it was fun to needle the bartender, for
She had on a New England jersey and cap.
"Why does she like the Patriots? Is she

From Massachusetts or something?" I asked
The dude next to me, who turned out to be a
Lawyer of 24 years, "It's Tom Brady, you know,
He's good looking, not like us!" He guffawed.

Chatting further, we agreed that those who are
Very pleasant to look at, not to mention to eat,
Will get all the breaks in life, though this won't
Necessarily promise success. "With this belly
And this chin, I'm handicapped, for sure, so if
The prosecutor is super appealing, I'm screwed,
But all I have to do is win over one juror, so if
I can work on one, if I can flirt with her, say,
Then I can get an acquittal or a hung jury."

The lawyer said he needed not go into
Whether his client was guilty or not. He only
Needed to work with the evidence, so if there's
Not enough to convict, that's that, "I don't ask
If he raped or killed. I only work with the evidence."
His career was on the upswing, and he even ran
For mayor of Bristol, until he got hooked on crack
At a heavyweight contender's birthday bash.
"Who are you talking about?" "I can't tell you."
"Local guy?" "Yeah." "Timmy?" He grinned.

Though never mayor of Bristol, the lawyer
Was a sort of mayor of Jack's, for he knew
Everybody there and, what's more, wanted to
Make everyone happy, or so he said, "If I see
Anyone here looking sad, I must cheer him up.
What if someone's having suicidal thoughts and
There's no one to talk to? That's why I talked to you.
Not that you're suicidal or anything, or maybe you are.
See that guy outside in the wheelchair? He lost his toes,
Thanks to frostbite. He's homeless," and with that,
The lawyer went outside to greet the toeless man.

So what are you missing, exactly? You can tell me.
I'll show you my gaps if you reveal your gashes.
Put your hand here. Yeah, like that. Easy! Can you
Feel what's gone? There used to be quite a lot there.
Boo coo dinky dow! Lotsa madness! Lotsa madness!
Ending, I'll give you some crucial information. Although
A can of Busch is only $1.50 here, it's not the best deal,
For a pint of Yuengling, which is much better, is only $2.

Dick Seeth, Moe and Woman Drinking Nothing

Illness forces a sharpening
Of self-definition, and so can
Argument. Some fights, though,
Are so stupid that the only solution
Is to walk away. Vietnamese proverb:
"Argue with a smart man, can't win.
Argue with a stupid man, can't stop."

Dick Seeth, let's just call him that, derives
Enormous pleasure from conflict, which
Empowers him. Without constant war,
He's bloodless and limp, a loser, which
He is, frankly, for there's no art or,
More importantly, love in his music.
Hiding behind posts, he shoots bile.

There are Dick Seeths all over, but the world
Is not, in fact, overrun by them, so yesterday,
I went up to Kensington to connect with a
Saner and sweeter humanity, and besides,
A pitcher of Yuengling at Jack's Famous Bar
Is only $3.75, and a cheesesteak four bucks.

With prices like that, the place was packed,
As usual, but I managed to find a stool, so
Let's listen to Moe, to my right, "I'm 73.
When I was 17, I got my first and only job,
Working at Globe Dye Works. They gave me
Tasks no one else wanted to do, and for that,
They paid me $6 an hour, which was excellent

Money way back then. I stayed for 18 ½ years.
What have I done since? Nothing! I survived on
Welfare and odd jobs. Now I'm on Social Security.

I get a grand each month. My landlord takes 400,
I have a room, with my own TV and ice box, but
I never cook, really. I eat here. One cheesesteak
Is usually enough for an entire day. I spend more
On beer," Moe laughed, "but if I'm out of cash,
I can borrow or I just don't drink. I stay home
To watch TV or listen to my radio. It's no big deal.

Yes, I've been married, but that was so long ago.
It only lasted six months! I was a virgin,
And she was pregnant, but I was pretty sure
It wasn't my child. We only did it once or twice,
But my mom and dad said, 'If you slept with her,
You should marry her,' so I did, but we argued
All the time. In the beginning, I gave her half
Of each paycheck, then I stopped. I didn't care.
I don't even know the kid's name. He wasn't mine.

I never remarried, never even came close.
The love of my life is in heaven," and Moe pointed
To the copper ceiling. Fully expecting him
To answer, "Mary. The Virgin Mary," I asked
For her name. "Bobbie," Moe said. "She died
At thirty-five, in her sleep. I still don't know why.
We were only together two years. It was love
At first sight, but she was married, you know.
In fact, it's her husband who knocked on my door
To tell me Bobbie had died. He knew about us.

Everybody did. He didn't mind. Maybe he also
Had a lover. Bobbie and I loved each other, but
It wasn't about sex. I was much older, you know.
How old? Let's see, she only died four years ago,
So I was 67 when I met her. It wasn't about sex.
In fact, we only did it maybe once or twice.
Sex is not that important to me. I've been
To a prostitute once or twice, also, and
I didn't really care for it. I was really drunk.

You don't have to do what everybody's doing.
I don't vote either. Don't believe in it. They always
Promise you this and that, then do whatever. I've
Only voted once. I voted for Kennedy, and that's
Mostly because he was Irish." Moe laughed.

By this point, I was on my second pitcher.
Behind the bar, beadworks by a bartender.
Of flowers, they cost 20 or 30 bucks.
On television, the Sixers were trying to
Not lose 27 consecutive games. I'm serious.
To my left, a woman of about 65, wearing a
Lidded knit cap, two coats, purple nail polish and
Chowing on cheese fries from Crown Chicken.
"Don't ever get fish sticks there," she advised.
"They're the size of French fries. I remember
Ordering them when Madonna was singing
During the Super Bowl. These are all right."
She kept talking to herself when not draining
Her empty mug. "Hey, you're drinking nothing!"
Without turning to me, she replied, "I know."
It was pouring when I left Jack's, but I was already

Feeling much cleaner, and so far removed from
The stench of those whose rage obscures.

Parking Tickets and Sex After Sixty

Two parking tickets for Patty in one day
Will set her back $102, so that's 12 hours
Of lost wage and tips, bartending at Jack's.
Looking hurt, the 67-year-old laments, "That's
My regular spot! I'll go to City Hall to fight it."
"But that's a lot of wasted time. Patty, what if
You just don't pay?" Carless, I'm ignorant here.

"They'll probably put me in jail. I don't need that."
"You've never been locked up?" "No, but many
Of the people who come in here have. I've heard
Enough about it." On TV, there's a Little League
World Series game on. Nobody's watching.
I'm on my second pitcher of Yuengling.

Mel, the owner, is at the far end of life
And a blur from where I sit. Earlier,
Patty has ticked off all the states
She's been to. She wants to see more,
"Before I need a seeing-eye dog."

"Patty, I hear there's a lot of sex in prison."
"Oh yeah? Maybe I should go then!
At least I'll get something out of it.
I haven't been laid in ten years!"
"Lots of gay sex," a Vietnam vet chimes in.

“Oh no, no, I don’t need no lezzie.”
“It’s not too bad with a strap on,” I grin.
“No, no, Sir, I want the real thing.”
Staring at me hard, she then growls, “I’ve
Been fucked plenty the last two years,
But with my pants on.” As you get older,

Your body becomes like a nebulous sack
Sheltering your shame-faced griefs, so that
They get even more confused each time
You’re hugged without your clothes on.
Trapped water is sloshing over bones.
Your genitals slacken, fade then retire.
Even when cajoled with heart, they doze.
Still, the eel grass sometimes dance.

Ars Alcoholica

Tit for Tat, “I was wondering why it seems
That a majority of your interviews take place
In bars? Is it because there is where one can
More easily connect with a cross section of
The local public, or is it something else?
As one who has spent very little time
Hanging out in bars, it just seems that whole
Other cross sections of the ‘America’ you seek
Out and expose are not appearing in your work.
I do have to admit, that like your most aggressive
Detractor, these pieces seemingly appear,
And I have read many of your pieces, more
Monochromatic, not very inclusive of other
Potential sources for thought and discovery.”

Me, “If you have limited time in a town
In which you know nobody, you go
To a public place where people gather
And in the United States, that’s a bar.

If I had the means, I’d infiltrate other venues,
But I don’t. I don’t get paid for my articles,
Though people Paypal me money to support
My wandering. If you want me to write
From more pricey haunts, you’re welcome
To bankroll me, but if you’re not inclined, then
This is what I have to offer. Working class people
Meet in bars, so even if I wasn’t writing Postcards,

I'd go to bars. The working class, underemployed
And unemployed don't go to concerts, art openings,
Fashion shows or golf courses. They hang out
In cheap bars, often for many hours at a time.

They don't care for the bar's decors or
How many beers it has, they just want
A place to sit and talk with their similars,
And when in a bar, they certainly don't
Talk about the bar itself, but everything
Outside of it, so if you find their stories
Monochromatic, then I'm afraid there is
Something wrong with your vision, for I
Can never find people's lives monochromatic.
Ten thousand more nights in bars would be
No waste of time, if I could soak in anecdotes
About the joys and sorrows of their existence,
Which is also my lot in life, though not,
Apparently, where you're coming from.

The thin walleted also go to bars to get out
Of their cramped quarters, especially if all
They have is a room in a shared apartment.
A crappy bar, then, becomes their communal
Living room, and a luxurious one at that, since
It has pictures on walls, free music and
Televisions showing sports, which many
Can no longer watch at home, not since
They canceled their cable subscription.

Finally, there's a sign in Di Nic's, a bar
Not too far from my front door, 'Never trust
A man who doesn't drink,' and beyond the
Jokey inducement to alcoholism, it's a
Admonishment against rejecting what
Every other man and woman is doing.
In many cultures, there are no separate plates
At meal times, so you simply eat and drink what
Everybody else is eating and drinking. If they
Drink sake, chianti or thin beer, you do that. If
They eat snakes, snails or blood pudding, you eat."

Bob

"I was born in Media, PA. I was
A carpenter, then a caddy. I'd make
Up to 125 bucks for four hours of work.
These rich guys would buy me a beer
At the halfway house. That's a place
To relax, just after the 9th hole, not a
Home for recovering junkies, drunks
Or criminals just sprung from prison. I

Know about that kind, too, for I simply
Love alcohol. First thing in the morning.
At 7 o'clock, I've got to have my drink.
I was also on crack for about five years,
And I've been on the streets for ten years,

In Atlantic City and Philly. I've been
Jumped about ten times. The back of my head
Is stapled. It's these black kids, about 15, 16,
They'd just hit you for no reason. Or they'd be
Talking to you, and suddenly they'd hit you.

I don't know where all that anger is coming from,
But I stay away from all black neighborhoods now.
I try not to wander from Center City. Black women,
Especially the older ones, give me money
Or food. They take care of me. I have a

15-year-old daughter with a black girlfriend.
I was with Diane for five years. That's my
Longest relationship ever. I haven't seen
Diane in years, and I don't even know
My daughter's name. I've never seen her.
She hates me, probably. I'm sure she does.

I've been in jail for vagrancy and
Public drunkenness, nothing violent.
I would never hurt anybody. I'm just
A friendly guy. When I was a kid,
My mom and dad hit me a lot, though.
My mom is still in Media, but I won't
Go see her. My dad is dead. Just last week,

I asked this guy for a quarter, and this man,
Who was really intelligent looking, you know,
And an office type. He said, 'Let me go
To the ATM,' and I thought, 'Shit, man,
Why is he going to the ATM for a quarter?'
But then he returned and gave me
200 bucks! I couldn't fuckin' believe it!
I'm still spending it. When I can't afford gin,

I drink mouthwash. The hardest part is
Getting that shit down, because it is nasty.
It says so right on the bottle, 'Do not swallow.'
But if you can keep it down, it will keep you
Pretty damn buzzed for four or five hours."

Bob wore green hospital pants and pale blue gown.
As we were talking, Bob would wave at cars.
Some drivers would wave back. A double decker
Tourist bus appeared, so Bob grinned and waved.
A tourist waved back. Both Bob and I thought
This was hilarious. Welcome to Philadelphia!
Before leaving Bob, I said, "You know you were
Walking around with your ass showing! You should
Go to that church over there and get some clothes."

"My ass was showing?!"

"Yeah, man, you should go to the church."

"Yeah, I know where that church is."

Wayne Says

Each month, each Chinese is paid \$12.50,
Which he must spend by the 15th, for if
He's caught with any money after the 15th,
He'd be shot. It's a capital crime. Also, if
He's caught with, say, \$12.51 at any time,
He'd also be killed. A Chinese doesn't really
Need any money, since the government gives
Everyone three meals and a cot, though they
Must work 24 hours a day. It's Communism.

Here we don't have Communism, so I buy
These hot dogs from the Dollar Store. They're big,
Just like kielbasi! Eight for a dollar. You don't even
Need to cook them. I eat them like lunch meat.
One thing, though, too many hot dogs will give you
Butt cancer. I'm sixty-six years old, and I don't need
My ass all torn up because I ate too many hot dogs.

I don't mind sleeping outside. It's like camping.
I had an apartment in this house, paid \$360,
Shared it with seven other knuckleheads.
Most of them were cool, though, but one guy
Would never flush the toilet, and never close
The shower curtain, so water would be all over.
Man, it was gross. He said he was germaphobic,
So he wouldn't touch the toilet, any part of it.

With so many guys in one place, you'll have
Disagreements every now and then. One time,
This seven footer came at me, so I stabbed him,

But my knife broke, so nothing happened to him.
He lunged at me again, but I had three darts, so
He backed off. Why did I have three darts on me?
Well, you don't know what I have on me, do you?

I know how to protect myself, but I'm not violent.
I went to college. I wanted to study business, but
My ma said, "Business ain't nothing but a way for
White people to rip off black people," so I switched
To music. I know how to play the guitar and piano.
I wrote songs, but I don't remember any of them.

We only need one educational system,
But Catholics have their own schools, so
The country is divided. Catholics don't like
Anybody who isn't a Catholic, and that's why
Nothing works in this country. We're divided.
Take the war, for example. We've been fighting
Ten years against people with nothing, against
Cavemen with only a few guns and a couple
Of hand grenades, while we have all these planes
And aircraft carriers, you know, the whole shebang,
But we still can't goddamn win. We're divided.

The city is falling apart, but Nutter can't get
Anything done, because he's a Catholic and
Obama is not. He can't just call up Obama and
Say, "Send us a hundred trillion zillion dollars!"

Flippant in El Paso

A cell at the De Soto Hotel costs
$199 a week, $399 a month,
But there's a ghost who stays free.
Sweet looking, she's probably not even
Sixteen-years-old. Anticipating
Whatever you're about to say, this ghost
Will whisper, with ticklish, hot breath
Tunneling into your ear, "So what?"

Philosophical in El Paso

If I lived in El Paso, The Tap would be my bar.
With $3 beer and $4 burrito, how can you go wrong?
For variety, there's a dodgy Chinese joint next door.

By The Tap, I met a homeless dude from Detroit
With a diamond tattoo between eyes. Twenty-eight-years old,
He has had one real job in life at 18, working at a factory
For $10 an hour, with his biggest accomplishment to date
The fact that he's been off heroin for two years. In Tucson,
He hooked up with some girl for two nights, "The best pussy
I've ever had, and it's not like I get that much pussy.
Just look at me!" Elated, he went out to get some beer
And was promptly hit by a car, resulting in a cracked hip
And a broken shin. Hence him limping now on a crutch.

"The next time you get great pussy, just pretend," I said,
"It's just nothing, that it's no big deal. That way, you won't
Get hit by a car, 'cause as soon as you enjoy something
Too much, see, shit will surely happen. Major shit!"
"I don't know if you can put it like that
Because, when it comes right down to it,
They're all about the same, if you ask me."

"So it wasn't really worth it, was it?"

"No, it wasn't, but I don't see the connection."

"Of course, there was. You congratulated yourself,
Got a little too high, so shit had to happen. Maybe
It would have been worth it if you were hit by a moped

Instead of a car? What kind of a car was it?" I asked.

"Just a sedan, but listen, dude, I don't even
Think a moped would have been worth it."

All men, except me, of course, are abject. “I’d eat
A mile of her shit just to see where it came from.”
Who said that? A man said that. An English speaker.
All men, except me, have said that. I just said that.

San Antonio

Tourists and vagrants roaming downtown
Near midnight. One fight, two arrests. Cops
Walking and riding in vans, cars and on bikes.
A pool table in a barber shop. Free mug of beer

With each haircut. In the window of vast liquor store,
A gallery of shoplifters caught by surveillance cameras.
Rat to get your Ben Franklin. "I know him! He my cuz!"

Shoved down jean crotch, a fifth of whiskey will shoo away
Those bank bailout, Federal Reserves blues. Black dude,

"Are you Japanese?" "No, Vietnamese." "Oh yeah?
I was in the navy. Okinawa." He was around 45, tired-
As-shit looking, yet edgy. It was dark, warm and I had
Just gotten off the train. On me, nearly 3,000 dollars

Of camera equipment. Feet away, a long form slept
In a recessed entrance. "Hey, man, I'm in shape,"
My new friend volunteered. "I'll do twenty pushups
For you if you give me three bucks."

Approaching Chicago

On train, a young man pulled up his T-shirt
To show pubic hair besieging belly button.
"I'm half French, see? You wouldn't see that
On a regular Vietnamese guy, would you?"

He was traveling to Colorado to work on a ski resort.
He had been making out to some girl he had just met.
He was thinking of returning to her, after our chat.

Should we make out or in? It is commonly said
That the boy should wear baggy jeans, to not
Compliment the girl too openly. The naked face
Can be most intensely erotic, alarming even long
Married spouses, sleeping in separate beds.

A man comes to yet another lascivious city.
Open faces flit by. He does business by day.
Night, he enters a bar hopeful and determined,
But of course, nothing happens, so he returns
To the wrong hotel room, alas. Finally, someone
Is waiting there for him, unbidden. Blind drunk,
He interprets this as a divine gift, a belated
Vindication of his own mortal worth. How
Did she manage to enter his room and why?

We passed Gary, Indiana, then into the South Side.
Impressive ruins of factories, row houses, an empty
Basketball court. It was gray, drizzling. In my twenties,
I wanted to work as baggage handler for Midway Airlines.

Stupid, I didn't even know they would give me a drug test,
So I smoked pot the day before they flew me to Chicago
For a damn drug test. Funny, but I wasn't even a pothead.

"You know what's funny about us Vietnamese?
We love our cars and our big flat screen TVs,
But there's nothing else in the fuckin' house!
These guys drive nice cars, then go home
And eat instant noodles each damn night!"

"Nice red cars," I interjected.

"Yeah, nice red cars. Hey, you know
What's my favorite instant noodles?"

"What?"

"Ma ma," he said, with a clear pause
Between syllables. To make sure
I got it, he said it again, "Ma ma."

Dying, say, from shrapnel, a man,
Craving instant noodles, no less,
Would utter with his last breath,

"Ma ma."

Wolf Point's Baddest Bar

On Water Hole's outside wall,
A cowboy and Indian relax,
At a placid pond, at dusk.

Inside, bar stools are bolted
To the floor, to prevent them
From being lifted and swung at any
Assiniboine, Sioux, Paleface or whoever
Talks or acts wrong, according to
The judgment of Budweiser.

Once, I swear, an obnoxious Navy Seal
Got his ass kicked, then chased out.
It's not true, though, that he ran
All the way to Cape Disappointment,
A spectacular park with lighthouse
In Washington State, facing Japan.

It must be said, though, that men
Are mostly cowards. They almost
Never fight one-on-one. Even faced
With a one-armed midget, most men
Will hesitate, then call for backup,
If not a massive air strike that ends
With the midget intact and defiant,
But the rest of wherever wiped out.

Before we lunge at each other's throats, friend,
Let's play a mellow game of pool. We'll share
This light broom stick as cue, since you won't
Need but a few stitches when I whack it
Upside your soul's shack, or you mine.

As toxic junk washes ashore, seals hack
While the aimless and idle bum beer.
Contentment is a mug in Water Hole,
With the future merely a foot away.

Why Can't We Be Everywhere at Once?

Born in Boring, Oregon, he dreamt for decades
Of Celebration, Florida, but after moving there,
He soon returned to Boring, Oregon because
Celebration, he realized, wasn't all that.

Somebody ought to establish a writers' colony
At Cape Disappointment, Washington. Corn dogs
For breakfast, lunch, dinner and late night snack.

Spending her entire life in Sweet Home, Oregon,
She never visited Vida, just 57 miles away,
An hour and eighteen minutes driving, if
You're not too eager for the end. "I've heard
About that place," she said to her husband,
Her fork stuck in the mashed potato, her face

Worn and pleading. "I wouldn't fuss over it, Midge.
We ain't never going there." Near Ashland,
There's the Dead Indian Memorial Highway.
After death, you can be in Celebration and
Boring at the same time. Deceased, you can
Absolutely be nowhere all the damn time.

Hinsdale, Montana

Since you ask, I'd say we're hard working,
Don't care for surface and trusting. Here,
Your words are like the words of God.
If you lie once, people will remember.

Our town did well during the Vietnam War
Because of the Glasgow Air Force Base.
That's where I met my husband, by the way.
We used to have three bars, two grocery stores,
Two hotels and even a car dealership. Now,
There are just Stoughie's Bar and Grill and a
New coffee shop, Sweet Memories. We're down
To 217 people, and everyone's white except
For five Indians and two Mexicans.
Also, farming isn't what it used to be.

Our big social event of the year is the
Street dance, BBQ, high school reunion
And rodeo around the Fourth of July.
A country band would play, but mostly
We just visit each other and chatter.
You can fish for walleyes in the Milk River.

My mother is 90. When she graduated
From high school, her class had 110 kids.
Mine only had 12, and this year's seniors
Were just four girls and a boy. There was
Another boy, but he died in a car crash.

Reading McCook

"God Bless America banner is $8.99."
"Bronze eagle to be raffled by art guild."
"BBQ tastes best with family."
"Free haircuts for a year!!! Enter to win."

Nourished, fortified and encouraged by
Copious cowpies, corpulent flies blunder,
Dart then land on your lips as if you're dead.
In their pens, cattle lament, sigh, fart and
Regurgitate fond memories. I wouldn't mind
Me a steak right about now, though with my
Budget, Chinese is hot and decent enough,
Except there's a sign, "Due to food shortage,
We will be closed Monday and Tuesday."

The Royal Buffet is built like a joke
Section of the Great Wall. What
Can they possibly be out of? Soy sauce,
Hoisin sauce, oyster sauce or MSG?
Working a serious wok requires two arms
And even your knee, for the gas lever.
As you labor, flames lick your crotch.

Nudged along by history, infrastructure,
Hunger and chance, I end up shading
My eyes to look at a showroom gravestone
That flaunts laser engraved tractor, barn and

Two turkeys, with the cock spreading feathers.
Thanks to technology, even a peasant
Can be interred ostentatiously. Once
A year, a nylon flag can be planted,
Like an asterisk, onto his memory.

Flags drape dead men and a dying
Nation that's not going down without
Shooting, bombing, droning and voting.
Flags are all over McCook. In a window,
A teddy bear is togged like a soldier.
Another cub fills a patriotic tub.
On a bench, a silhouette of a soldier
Kneels next to a Christian grave. Above him,
There is an eagle, a flag and a poem that

Starts, "Don't weep for me / Oh land of the free.
When it was my time to fall / Twas
For my country's call." It finishes,
"And in her freedom and her courage /
I'll continue to live." At the theater,
A playbill announces a 9/11 play
To benefit the McCook Fire Department.
On a porch, a molded resin flag has yellowed.

Tramping in the sun for hours, my yellowness
Reverts to red. Red enough, I need beer,
So I ask the white mailman, "Sir, where can I
Get a drink around here? Like, a tavern?"

"Old Sarge's is where you need to go! Good luck!"
Unsure if I need fortune to get there or
Simply to get sloshed there, I barge in.

Describing a late 19th century
Nebraska town, Willa Cather,
"The dwelling-houses were set about
Haphazard on the tough prairie sod; some
Of them looked as if they had been moved
In overnight, and others as if they were
Straying off by themselves, headed
Straight for the open plain."

Thirteen decades later, the buildings
Appear provisionally more permanent,
But with a persistent drought, the soil
Is again truculent, so that these burgs
May just be blown away, like dead bugs.
Tallgrass and buffaloes counterattack.
Indians, punks and failed writers kick weeds.
Soon enough, then, there will be fewer shacks
On these prairies. Meanwhile, though, descendants

Of homesteaders are swilling Bud,
Bud Lite and Miller all around me.
One guy is sucking with a tiny straw
His one-dollar-shot special. I shout,
"Hey, what is that you're drinking?"
We chitchat. He asks back, "What

Are you doing in town?" "I've never
Been to Nebraska, outside of a few
Hours in Omaha, so that doesn't count."

Eyes stern, he delivers, "There's something
You're not telling me!" Then, to another,
"Look at his eyes!" Meaning my eyes,
Mind and whatever else are not normal
To his round, red eyes. Still drunker, he asks,
"When are you leaving?" "In a few hours,"
I say, "Tonight." "Good, we don't need
More of your kind around!" "What kind?!"
The cheap shot drinker doesn't answer.

Drumbeating for conquest, Walt Whitman
In "Pioneers! O Pioneers!" sought to
Galvanize "O you youths, western youths"
Of his "resistless, restless race!" His kind.
"Swift! to the head of the army!–swift!"
From Jamestown on, this land was cleared
And ethnic cleansed for a specific kind.

Buffalo Bill killed 4,000 bisons.
Tourists shot bisons from moving trains.
To slaughter bisons is to wipe out Indians.
Blanched bison skulls rose up to the moon.
This world had to be reshaped and whitewashed.
With the beast gone, McCook High School's
Football team is called the Bisons, of course.

It must be said, though, the unkind
Kind-focused man is not emblematic
Of McCook. Others are much more friendly.
Let's listen to 50-year-old Jason,
"I've worked on oil rigs in Colorado,
But not North Dakota, since my bones
Can't deal with the extreme cold. Colorado
Is cold enough, but it doesn't get to thirty
Or forty degrees below zero. I hope
To move to the Gulf Coast soon. I've never
Seen the ocean. I grew up very poor."

Half a mile away, there's Club Paradise,
With a beach scene on its sign. McCook is
Nearly a thousand miles from salt water.
Maybe there's a Hail Storms and Blizzards Bar
In Miami, with a snowplow on its sign?

Gaunt, bespectacled, smooth jowled, unsmiling,
Seventy-eight-year-old Will, "I've driven trucks
My entire working life, been to every state,
But I like my home state, Nebraska, best.
In fact, everything East of the Ohio River
Can go to hell or sink into the damn sea!
I'm still working because me and my wife
Don't want to live on less. I'll retire at 80."

The longer you linger, the more each street
And street lamp will gossip behind your back,
So an old man can choose to embrace
His history, as woven into a spot,
Or he can try to shun it, but inside
Each person, the fallen houses still stand.
That said, Nebraska can't be more home
Than any place else, for all of our edifices
Have only been blown here a few beers ago,
And with the next cheap shot, knocked down.
This mirage is conjured up by much fluids
Being sucked deliriously from raped earth.

Finally, a poster skeleton lifts
The venetian blinds, then two doors down,
On a sweatshirt, there's a football helmeted
Skull and crossbones, "A tradition
Of toughness. Nebraska Corn Huskers."

Carla from Syracuse

I suppose I married the wrong man,
But I imagine it can't be too unusual.
My parents came from Italy. Foggia.
My dad was super strict. As long as
I lived at home, I had to be home
By midnight, and this lasted until I
Married at twenty-one. My husband
Was a nice boy until he returned
From serving in the Army. In Germany,
He picked up new ideas, like free love.

Though we dated again, I was actually
Happy when he moved to Houston, Texas.
One night, my husband called collect and said,
"Will you marry me?" He was drunk, I could tell.
My dad never liked him, my mom sobbed,
But still, I got out of the house, finally.
It was my first decision in life. For years,
I chose not to have children. I knew.

We ended up marrying for thirty-five years.
In fact, we got married twice, for only
A year and a half after our divorce,
He asked me to marry him again, and
I said yes, again, like a complete idiot.
Though it was the wrong life, I didn't know
Any other life, so I went back to it.

Now, I'm finally alone, and happy.
I have two grown, successful kids.
They're always trying to set me up,
But I tell them no, I'm really happy.
As for my regrets, they tell me, "Mom, if
You didn't marry dad, you wouldn't have us."

My husband has found another wife, and
Thank God, she's not younger, for that
Would really eat me up. As for my dad,
Who's dead, I don't blame him. He could
Only bring us up the way he was raised.

Sometimes I do go on dates, but I always
Say beforehand that it would only be
A dinner and a movie, and no more.
Well, maybe a quick hug at the very end.
People say my husband's wife is bipolar.
I've googled her, seen her face.

Harriet of Richmond

There is a Jefferson Pawn Shop, a Baptist church
In a converted car dealership, and a Nation of Islam mosque
In a former church, complete with a crucifix-topped steeple.

Seeing some Jesus exhortation in a thrift store, I walk in
And meet Harriet, a 64-year-old employee wearing brown,
Plastic glasses and a blue baseball cap. A transplanted
New Yorker, Harriet was a home care nurse for decades
Until one of her arms went weak, until she got old herself.

She's been married for 39 years, she beams.
Her husband is 76. "And I'll take care of him
Until the end. He won't be in any nursing home."
Though Jewish, she got married in a church,
To please her Irish husband. "At the ceremony,
The priest said I should wear my Star of David
Inside my dress, and I had on a white dress
Because I was a virgin. I said, 'I'll wear this
Inside my dress if you remove that cross
From the wall, behind you.'" Harriet's

First love was a man half Filipino,
Half Cambodian. The day before
Their wedding, he revealed he had a son.
He also warned, very sternly, that

Should anything happen to him,
Everything will go to this son.
Harriet told him to shove it.

Harriet and her husband were trying
To go from New York to Florida when
They ran out of cash in Richmond. They
Have also slept in shelters or outside.
On the yellow wall, a babe in a stroller
Reaches out to a hirsute dude in white
Tennis shoes, jacket and faded jeans.
"I tell you the truth, whatever you did
For one of the least of these brothers..."

Ethel in St. Louis

I have diabetes, and so did my mom.
After she retired, she just watched TV.
She hardly went outside, hardly moved.
"I've moved all my life. I'm tired of moving."
She had been a home nurse. She was tired,
And alone for twenty years. When dad died,
My mom didn't even go to the funeral.
She wouldn't have been able to take it.
She would have jumped right in. In fact,
She never visited his grave, not even once.

The oddest thing, though, happened when
She herself died. We called the cemetery
And was told the burial plot had been paid for,
And was right next to my dad's, too. I know
No one in my family arranged that. It must
Have been a clerical mistake on their part,
But it's perfect. I think my dad did it.

Toronto

Draped in an East Indian outfit, a young woman
Belted out a Russian song, at the Russia
Festival in Dundas Square, and no one
Seemed bemused. This is Toronto.

In an Old York park, a dozen books
On the grass–Robin Rice, Anne Tyler,
Stephen King, you know, the usual
Bullshit. How sweet it was that no one
Had bothered to pick these up, but then, I thought,
Maybe they already own these titles. What if

bpNichol had been scattered, like this, as gifts
Or trash. They would probably remain there
For the next millennium or two. Speaking
Of orphaned language, I collided with

"WE SERVE ALL DAY DIM SUM," not
To be confused with "WE SERVE
DIM SUM ALL DAY." Maybe they meant
"WE SERVE DAY-OLD DIM SUM."

Dim sum means "to touch the heart,"
By the way, and all I ever wanted was
To massage your core with syllables.

On King Street, I saw, quite suddenly,
A blown-up comic with "La ferita
Continua a sanguinare." The wound
Continues to bleed, and the only
Response to that is "Basta! Basta!
Do you want to focus or not? Let us
Focus. You and me, let us focus."

Make it Swift

Many insist that the modern toilet
Is a male figure, a middle-aged grump
Complaining endlessly about what did
Or didn't happen in his sighful life. Others
Will counter that the commode is actually
Quite a lovely lady, with enviable curves.
But what about that lid on her mouth?

"Other women are so envious of me.
I can't sleep a wink, without worrying
That your wife, for example, will sneak
In here to steal my lid, and snap it onto
Her own lovely yet incomplete mouth."

This poem is so full of it.
And I'm so full of it, being a
Sighful middle-aged creep. Ah!

But why do we read and digest
At the same time, desecrating
Both reasonably excusable acts?
So put this non-poem down, please,
And finish musing in relative peace.

Self-Love is Blind

A man missed his dead wife so much. When
Remarrying, he insisted that his second wife
Changed her name to match the first. Of course,
He was careful to find a woman who resembled
His gone sweetie as much as possible. He did
Cheat some, however, since the woman he chose
Approximated his first wife in early youth, and not
Late middle age, the age at which she died. This
Ain't a bad deal, he thought. Though the second
Wife's face was nearly that of the first, maybe even
Slightly more pretty, her proportions were certainly
Lesser. A detail here, there and everywhere, really,
Were also off. With clothing, these liabilities
And deficits were hardly noticeable, but, in bed,
Well, there was the truth and nothing but the truth.
These discrepancies became so disturbing that
He would ask her, rather indelicately, to keep
As much clothes on as possible as they embraced.
Finally, he had to insist that she visit a renown
Plastic surgeon which he had found online
After much googling and aggressive querying
In beauty forums, under the name Sue. After
A series of discreet or brazen augmentations,
Tucks, lifts, obscure tightening, dermabrasion,
Tautening, thermolysis and laser treatments,
She was finally home, That is, his dead wife
Finally reappeared.

Air Duct to Air Duct

To kiss is to threaten
To eat someone without
Actually chewing and swallowing.
It is also to wed digestive tracts,
Meaning the ultimate expression
Of intimacy, no less than
Having two assholes welded
Together, otherwise
Known as marriage.

Suing God

After decades of deliberation, I want to
Sue God for my ridiculously bad teeth. What is
The statute of limitation on crooked teeth, anyway?
Who cares? I'll sue. If successful, I'll move on down
The list of my other physical and mental deformations.

Chatting with Greg Martino, director of career service
At an art school, I said, "I've seen a dentist just once
In thirty years." "That's incredible!" We were talking
About the sacrifices and pitfalls of trying to be an artist
If one isn't a trust fund kid. "My biggest fear was being
Irrelevant. I didn't want to give up everything just to suck,
But of course that's always the safest bet." Thank God,

I have these actionable teeth to meditate on. They keep me
Mucking in mortality, and makes hubris nearly impossible,
Though I preen often enough, despite the sad emblem
And monument to my intrinsic worth, my incisors.

Yet Another

The ugliest man alive.
The most hideous woman,
Dead or alive. (I want *her*.)
Even the prettiest woman,
Even the most God-like man.
How else can I put it? Where
Should I put *this*, exactly?
Not here, soldier...

Yet another transsexual beggar
With his useless genitals tied with
A pretty knot round his neck, like
Some kind of well-ironed irony.

In Wichita and not Wenatchee,
I met a soul with a life-size
Life stuck on his fuckin' life.
(I know, I know, obscenity
Means poverty of language.)
I am poor, stinky and stupid.

Say something you've never uttered.
Do something weird, why don't you?
Once, if I remember well, my life was
A feast of cable TV and web porn.

This is my mother, a month before
She tricked me into marriage, her belly
Already bulging with my stillborn father.

Baby

for Mieko Kawakami

Day by day, the baby grows, which can only mean that, day by day, the mother is being lowered into the grave. Thus, she wills that her baby should remain forever the size of a hamster.

As the infant ages, the mother rejuvenates, but they resist the temptation to mate after so many years. Now, mother is a screaming newborn, and the child is a frowning parent to its own mom. Sighing, it shakes its head at that blind thrust towards procreation.

Soon as her baby is born, she knows it's already much wiser than her. Judging her with its seasoned eyes, her baby ticks off countless physical, intellectual and moral shortcomings. I should snuff you out right now, she contemplates, before you become even more insufferable.

For many years, maybe even decades, her baby can only make nonsensical sounds. This, she interprets as infinite mercy on her baby's part, for she lives in constant terror of what it will finally utter with its first fully-formed sentence.

One gorgeous morning, she wakes up screaming because her baby has been snatched from her, most violently, in the middle of the night, then she realizes, with an uproarious laugh, that she never even had a baby. With no husband, a virgin, she's only a child herself. She is the baby.

Anything Else?

In Philly, there was a man who pushed pills
And performed late term terminations.
Many were born into the toilet, to be
Fished out and killed, scissored
Through the neck. Over decades,
This man killed countless. Those
Who weren't killed immediately
Had a few minutes of life, but most
Lived for merely seconds, spent
Mostly in their first and last crapper.

Mere is French for mother.
Mare means sea in Italian.

I was dumped from one water
Into another. I went from a tight
Yet vast enough sea, my mother,
Into a public ocean, the toilet.
Lone boat in a shitty womb, I
Learnt how to sculpt tampons, turds
And toilet paper into SOS. Before
I had my first milk, I experienced a
Golden shower. Give it to me, mom!
Because of some unfortunate fucking,
I became inexorably flushable, if only
I wasn't already too big. I felt a pair
Of firm hands rescuing me, thank god,
But that was that. I stopped seeing.

I Love You

You know how it is, their idea
Of paradise is being born a sagging,
Wrinkled and stinking corpse, only
To mature into an earnest, firm and
Sexually anarchistic youth, then die
As a manure-spewing and shrieking
Meat package, being inserted into the
Grave of your one true love and hate.

Two Men

In the men’s room at Market East,
A commuter train station, I noticed
A wheelchair in front of a stall, then
I heard, “I can't believe it. Why? Why
Would you fuck the nigger?! Fuck me!
Why would you do that? Fuck me!
Why would you fuck the nigger?!”
And on and on along that vein. Then

Washing my hands, I could see, reflected
In the mirror, the sitting lamenter. With his
Eyes shut and one hand on his forehead,
He was a black man of at least 55.

Whits

Before he could tongue her, one of his teeth
Fell out. "That's OK," he winked at his stale
Yet chirpy stablemate, "I still have plenty left."
As if to prove it, he spat out a stringy and
Bloody assortment, then counted to ten
Before losing interest. He popped them back.

They kissed for the longest time, maybe even
A bit longer, since they had already paid too much,
You see, and had to get the most out of this swindle.
They had to milk it *by any means necessary*. "This

Is way overrated," she grimaced. "Aren't you gonna
Ask what I've been reading? It's not Jonathan Swift,
That's for sure. I mean, I like poetry and everything,
But soon as I bite into one... " "You just wish you hadn't,"

He finished the sentence for her. Speaking of sentences,
Some should be as long as the most tedious bridge
You will ever encounter, while others could be as brief
As this sunshiny life, and it always matters. Many whits.

Wrong Tool Man

Out of some desperate
Political, philosophical
And moral conviction, he uses
Scissors as toothpicks,
Books as footrests or chairs,
Hotels as sexy morgues,
Genitals as ghost limbs,
Brain as bowels,
Shakespeare as André Breton,
Life as afterlife,
Earth as moon.

Hard

Though all names are gaseous, and soon,
Mercifully, to be blown away, it's still better
To have a minty moniker than to be cursed,
Even after death, by one's creditors and marks.

Silly old Jew, how can your last breath trump
Your howling birth, for even a quick slant
Of sunshine is worth it, though you end up toast.

Precocious, he'd rather linger at open caskets
Than slobber at orgies, not that there's any.
Even before the clumsy and anxious undressing,
They might flee, leaving you to touch yourself.
Unlike corpses, lovers don't stay put. Come,

Let's tickle each other before we're hard.
Boozing, we sling tosh, but that's fine, for
Deadened faces can't cheer up the damp,
Mutely suffering yet, at times, perky parts.

With a tube down his throat, the sick man dreams
Of pho with raw and cooked beef, and brisket,
While in a darkened room, a young man stares
Very hard at miraculous strangers. Sleepless,
She imagines much nudging, lapping and kissing.
Only in the mind does life spread out fully. As
The young man cleans his crotch, the corpse
Is washed, then incinerated. She too washes.

Mare Mere

Bend down, everything's under there.
Lift up that ocean, and see for yourself.
Is it possible to commit worse violence
Against our vast mama, whom we gag with
Swirling plastic, spew oil and corexit stew,
Vomit irradiated slop into her lapping maw?

Welcome to Fukushima Sushi Takeout!
House specialty: Radiated Cesium Roll.
International Atomic Energy Agency approved.
Meet radiant chef, Naoto Kan. All you can't eat
Lunch, dinner and wake. Free goggles, mask,
Toothpick and industrial galoshes upon entry.

The Vietnamese word for country is water.
Which water are you from? Though I was born
In that water, I'll die in this water. To be together
Is to be in the same water, same womb. Come
Closer, mare mere, let's spend this longest night
Cuddling and spooning. Do we have a choice?

Neruda, however, thought the sea should
Be tamed and dominated. I translate
A chunk from his "Oda al Mare":

we'll enter you,
we'll chop the waves
with a knife made of fire,
on an electric horse
leaping over foam,
singing
we'll sink
until we touch the bottom
of your guts,
an atomic thread
will guard your shank,
we'll plant
in your deep garden
trees
of cement and steel,
we'll tie
your hands and feet,
on your skin man will walk,
spitting,
yanking in bunches,
building armatures,
mounting and taming you
to dominate your spirit.

Born next to the sea, even an extraordinarily
Smart man can claim to have never seen
His mama speak in her own language. Way,
Way down there, steel pricks are puncturing
Exhausted womb to bring back sick tidings.

Seagull Lecturing Bottom Dwelling Fish

What the fuck is wrong with you?
While everybody else is uplifting themselves,
You lie there, all day long, on the fuckin' bottom!
You make friends with dregs, tossed bottles and shit
As you stay clear of anyone who tries to help you.
You're terrified of a more enlightened existence!
You're just afraid of success, that's my verdict.
You adore the dark, the darker the better and
Don't even know how unhealthy your life is!
For years, I've been trying to help you, to lift you
Out of your briny hellhole, but I'm losing patience.
Soon as you see me, you burrow even deeper
Into your Dantesque abyss, your muck, your
madness.

Homelessness Starter Kit, $29.99.

For the myriad who were hustled
By a bank into an impossible mortgage,
Then foreclosed upon. For the long-retired
Yet taxed right out of their own homes.
For recent college grads who are jobless
Yet too dispirited to return to their nagging
Moms and pops. Or for those who were
Simply laid off for no good reason and
Are now roofless, here's a perfect gift
For this holiday: Two pieces of cardboard,
One to lie on, and one to create a begging
And/or protest sign. As a bonus, we'll include
A list of suggested messages, completely free:
WE ARE THE 99%, PREGNANT AND HUNGRY,
I HAD A STROKE, I AM A WAR VETERAN,
OCCUPY EVERYTHING DEMAND NOTHING, etc.
For a Magic Marker, please add $1.99.

Military Contractor Gear, $499.95.

For that aspiring mercenary in your family,
Now he can get off his couch and terrorize
Terrorists, without leaving his parents' home.

Armed with a knife, grenades, M9 pistol
And the latest Kalashnikov, the world's most
Reliable infantry rifle, not that toy gun, M-16
Piece of crap, your hired soldier can foray
Into his backyard and blast nasty holes
Into his dog, cat and lawn furniture.

Emboldened, he can venture into
Adjacent properties and kick down
His neighbors' doors in the dark and
Splatter them if they resist, or even if
They submit. There's no need for your
Deranged warrior to be bummed out over
The end of the Iraq War, since he can
Bring all of that exciting carnage home.

If bored with nightly mayhem, your contractor
Can step on an improvised explosive device
(At $79.95 extra, with only one needed, trust us)
And feel the thrills of having his lower half,
At least, shredded. Real life hired-guns
Don't get Purple Heart, but we'll ship you
An authentic looking one, at $4.99 extra.

Big Sis Sex Doll, $65.99, with $9.99 for handcuffs and $29.99 for TSA uniform.

Tired of Janet Napolitano rummaging
In your pants? Now you can get into hers.
This is no generic, almost life-size dummy
With the usual, traditional orifices in more
Or less the right places, or even that rarified,
Glasses-wearing and Emily Dickinson-quoting
Vinyl girlfriend. No, Siree! This is the Secretary
Of Homeland Security in face and person, her
Unique body shape extraordinarily rendered
By a world-renown, Chinese artisan, a classmate
And rival, no less, to the sculptor of that hulking
And fug ugly MLK statue on the Washington Mall.

Spiffy in your TSA outfit, you can intone
On your very first date, "This is merely procedural,
Ma'am," as you legally insert your creepy claws
Inside Janet's business pants and fondle her pubis,
Buttocks and more, with no foreplay whatsoever.
Why waste time? Like any sane person, she will
Squirm, grimace or even curse in a realistic,
Battery operated shriek, AA cells not included,
But should Janet resist your patriotic, post 9-11
Molestation, you can harden your voice and growl,
"I'll send you to Guantanamo, bitch!" before
You handcuff her and get really funky. Fun over,

You can waterboard Janet's face and gently wash
Her body with warm water and soap. Deflated,
She is compact enough to store in a back pocket
Until the next airport patdown and/or enhanced
Interrogation technique session.

Home Slot Machine, $199.99

With offshoring, American factories
Become hulking relics. Once the makers
Of high-quality merchandises, Americans
Now merely service or hustle each other,
Whether in investment banking, at street corner
Shell games or in casinos. Forty-one states now

Boast glittery gambling emporia, with these
Springing up even in an old church or a
Disused steel plant. It's not farfetched
To imagine a day when there are poker,
Blackjack, roulette and mahjong tables
Near every home. They'll have to be within
Walking distance, of course, since Americans
Will be too broke to afford car or gasoline.

Hell, it is probable that there will be a slot
Machine installed outside each dwelling, even
One of tarp or cardboard, where the mailbox
Used to be. The government won't deliver letters,
With the postal service long out of business,
But it will stop by regularly to collect coins

From your personal gambling contraption. Why not
Leap into the future, my friend, by having a slot
Machine right now in your living room? If you still
Have a living room, that is. Day or night, you can
Compulsively stuff your dwindling income into
This cartoon-decorated steel box, then crank

Its handle without consequence. As in a real
Casino, your money will be magically transferred
To unseen persons elsewhere. This mindless toy
Is tough enough to endure repeated kicks, bangs
Or even an atomic bomb, without showing any of
Your disappeared earning. With each $200 spent,
However, it will spit out a 25-cent coupon, to be
Spent at the low-end supermarket of your choice.

Obama's Dream

The latest crop of drones have artificial intelligence,
So they can decide for themselves who's the enemy,
And whether to kill or just maim him. They can also
Torture their target, by firing at his fingers or toes,
One by one, or an eye, or a nose at an angle, so

Only the schnozzle is knocked off, without the bullet
Entering the brain. Genitals can be shredded, but
Slowly, to maximize pain. All is well, until these drones
Enjoy killing so much, they'll shoot someone just for fun,
Or out of boredom, like a soldier might. By now,

Drones have well-developed personalities, with
The more immoral and ruthless rising up the hierarchy.
The nastiest, a drone that can kill thousands at once
While schmoozing, charming and joking, is declared
The President of the United States of America,

Except the country he leads, so to speak, is just
A fetid, desolate and charred wreck after so many
Decades of misrule and war. People, real people, weep
Joyful tears as the drone gives his inaugural speech,

While intellectuals trip over each other to compare this
Elegant and eloquent weapon to Washington, Jefferson,
Lincoln, FDR or Kennedy. Even in a dream, I'm irked
To go unmentioned as a precursor to this cool killer.

Poetry Sightings

It is Poetry Month again, but most Americans wouldn't know it, preoccupied as they are with forechecks, Mitt, Kim, Lady, Pippa and Doritos Locos Tacos. What a far cry from what Walt Whitman envisioned, since he actually thought our country would value poets more than any other. It has gotten worse and worse since his days. Just think of John Brown, for example, since Brown triggered an explosion of poetry, with hundreds of poems published in the immediate aftermath of his raid and hanging. Back then, Americans still considered poetry to be an essential response to, and perhaps even shaper of, national events and crises. Now, poems are completely irrelevant, and a major reason for this is the mass media. Americans are most indifferent to poetry because our country generates more nonsense and distraction than anybody else. Though shunned and drowned out, poetry still lurks across this land, however:

In New Orleans, two guys sit behind typewriters on a sidewalk in the exceedingly charming neighborhood of Marigny. Inspired by Jazz, no doubt, they will instantaneously write a poem on "your topic," and, get this, at "your price." Go ahead and try them, but don't go easy now. Demand that they write a poem on Grimm's law, gimcrackery, the Dust Bowl, viridity or the amazing life and death of Ioan Petru Culianu, for example, and pay them well, of course.

In Boulder, there is a smudgy facsimile of Walt Whitman wandering around, wearing sandwich boards that announce, "I'm Reverend Friendly–a poet and I know it. I earn my bread by reciting a poem I have stored in my head, But if you're too poor, I'll do it for free instead. Halleluiah, praise be to the Holy One!"

When the Reverend says one, he means the same poem each time, but sometimes not even that in its entirety, as when he forgot the final, killer stanza to Baudelaire's "To The Reader." After some nudging from me, however, Friendly finally belted out, with flecks of spittle spraying my poor face:

> Boredom! He smokes his hookah, while he dreams
> Of gibbets, weeping tears he cannot smother.
> You know this dainty monster, too, it seems –
> Hypocrite reader! – You! – My twin! – My brother!
>
> [translated by Roy Campbell]

In Boston, there is a young woman whose life is truly a poem. She said, "From the age of twelve, I've always wanted to be an animal," and that's why she goes barefoot and lives outside as much as possible.

Drifting around for the last four years, she has traveled as far north as Alaska, and as far south as New Mexico. In Montana, she slept outside in -20 degrees. She was staying with Occupy Boston until the police evicted their encampment from Dewey Square.

She has investigated the Transcendentalists and found them half-assed.

"If you want to be an animal, then Thoreau ain't shit," I said.

"Yes, Thoreau ain't shit."

In Chicago, there's a Poetry Garage, and, no, I'm not making this up. Why would I make it up? I'm too honest, earnest and anal retentive to make anything up, ever. The Poetry Garage is at 201 West Madison, and for a modest fee, say, $2,000 a month, you can park your miserable, beloved poem in the Poetry Garage, where no one, but no one, will ever proposition it, not that it's been getting lucky anyway, lately or ever. My primary and lifelong interest, however, is not in this Poetry Garage but in the cousined, digestively related Poetry Junk Yard, reputedly further West, where every life form, radiant or otherwise, goes to die, with its dreams, Hollywood or otherwise, never coming close to being fulfilled. Hey, but the road was fun and crippling! The Poetry Junk Yard is said to be larger than the Earth itself.

In Providence, some wise guy at Cafe Francaise has decided to scrawl some effete, literary hors d'œuvre on the chalk board each morning, and on March 11, 2011, at exactly 1:12PM, I was affronted with this nonsense from a guy I've never heard of: "Poetry begins when we look from the center outward–Ralph Waldo Emerson." This nutrition-free yet pestering nugget was promptly redeemed, however, by a lovely coda–and all codas are lovely, my dear, in its proper lighting and coupled with a carafe or six pack–right beneath it, "Today's Soup: Chicken Tortilla."

As we all know, Providence is home to excellent Brown University, an ivory Watts Tower that mostly benefits folks parachuted in from divers brown stones, cul-de-sacs and walled and moated communities. That is, they ain't quite germane to Providence itself, with its million Dunkin' Donuts and a few excellent Cambodian eateries. So here's the punch line: Brown pays only 2 million bucks of city tax yearly when it should cough up 19, which is exactly the deficit of corn syrup and transfat-mainlining Providence. Ah, but Brown has an excellent writing program!

Opening a Brown door to go outside, I nearly slammed into a white bearded and ushanka wearing character, so I shouted my standard greeting, "Yo, let's go for a beer!" But this Russian caricature dude was not impressed. Though he seemed crazy, he probably thought I was crazy. It turned out he was the take-no-prisoner Keith Waldrop. Just so you know now, Keith doesn't bullshit, and he has stopped going to poetry readings or lectures. He has enough poems in his head to last several millennia, so he has to use what little time he has left to hunker down and turn each one over, to examine each from all sides, to decide whether it belongs in the Poetry Garage or the Poetry Junk Yard.

In El Paso, there's a gentleman with a vaguely rhythmic specimen permanently lodged in his head. I found him at The Tap, a divey, old man's bar downtown. A retired Vietnam vet, he had spent 13 years in Juarez, but the increasing violence and extorting cops chased him back stateside. We did agree, though, that Juarez has its sweetness and charms. It's not just cops with assault rifles and flyers everywhere seeking loved ones. At any time of the day, it's more alive than El Paso, that's for sure. With its bustle and colors, Juarez reminded me very much of Vietnam, I told him, and he concurred, "But if they feel like shooting you, they'll shoot you right in the middle of a crowd. Even if it's sixteen bullets, they'll all hit you, with none hitting anybody else!"

After I admitted that I was more or less a writer, he said that he also wrote. He was a poet, to be more specific, "I've been writing since I was four!"

"Do you have any poem in your head you can write down for me?"

"Yes! In fact, I do. I'll write it down for you right now." And he immediately went at it.

Done, he motioned for the bartender to come over so he could declaim his poetry to her. She listened patiently, though without much comprehension, even if there was no Norteno music in the background, yet at the end, she beamed in relief and shouted, "That's beautiful!" Before scramming away.

As he handed his poem to me, he explained how he managed to compose it, "I wrote this after my first wet dream. Yes, my very first, when I was already in my 30's! I dreamt that I was back in Vietnam, and I was in a firefight, and it was one of those terrible firefights when you couldn't even think, when your mind went blank because you were so confused and terrified. My mind went blank, and I couldn't think at all, but suddenly the noises stopped, and I was in this hooch, and it was completely silent, and in walked six or seven Vietnamese women. You know, when I first got to Vietnam, I couldn't tell the women apart. The men, I could figure out, but the women all looked the same to me. I was sleeping with this one girl, and I thought I was in love with her, but then I couldn't tell if it was her I saw on the streets. Is that her? Is that her? Anyway, here I was in this dream, and in walked these Vietnamese women, and they were all beautiful, but I couldn't tell them apart, so I had to look at their legs. Suddenly, I could tell which woman was for me, because she had black legs!"

This vet was black, by the way, but as I started to comment how ironic it was that he couldn't tell Vietnamese apart, when racist whites, and Asians too, would say that they can't tell one black from another, he stopped me with volcanic irritation, "You have no rights to judge my feelings! This is my soul! My creativity! You're judging my art! You have no rights to judge my art!"

And with that, our conversation ended, but I still have his poem here. Like most, the chance of it being even slightly good or readable is very slim, but who am I to say? Nearly all of our poems are barely read now, much less in the future.

In Austin, someone has scrawled on the bathroom wall of a cafe on Congress Street, “I don’t know if you or I exist, but somewhere there are poems about us.”

CC FBI

As the FBI gutterpunk division entraps
Five guys with crude haircuts, anarchists
Supposedly, because anarchists are always
Guilty of everything, going back to Haymarket,
And beyond, we need a concrete poetry
For the true criminals to bite on. Eat this.

Or how about a poem that will explode
In the face of the corrupt, even if it kills
The poet as he's writing it. Swallow this.

As ship lists and drones fly, we
Don't need poetry as earworm,
But as tasseled cushion for ass
Of Goldman Sachs CEO, to blow
Up his rottenness, we demand

Poetry waterboarded onto the lying,
Smug and top-shelf mug of the Prez,
At a White House soiree, and beamed
From begging PBS, as foreclosed
Citizens cheer while spitting out
Microwaved Chef-Boy-a-Poem.

Funded by the maker of Prozac and Cialis,
American poetry puts you to sleep with a boner.
I mean, shit, you can't make shit like this up,
So it's high time for a John Brown poetry to surge

From the flooded basement of our cranium, as
Real John Browns sally forth to retake the real,
Rout nonsense and reclaim our definition.

*

To think is to act, now, so,
Like any foreign nation, you
Can also be preempted from
Your future crimes. If you don't
Believe me, just ask the FBI
Agent you're lying next to,
Under or above. He or she
Can kill you in the dark, in silence,
And that's no Middle Eastern joke.

Well, then, I'm a thought criminal,
A terrorist, since I fantasize always
About penning or zapping those who
Spend their lives sowing chaos,
Despair and wholesale horror.
Soon as I close my eyes, I see
Skyscrapers being imploded
And freefalling into their huge
Criminal footprints and scattering
Fraudulent investments and mortgages.

I fancy myself stepping over corpses
Of tax-dodging and looting CEOs,
War profiteers and propagandists,

The ones who keep feeding us lanky dogs
Dryhumping homing soldiers, but don't show
Those who are killed, maimed or tortured
By these same guys and gals next door.

Dumped from the imperial meat grinder,
They'll become your police or panhandle
From neocons and libtards, even Occupiers,
And though a terrorist, I'll give them a buck.
"Man, you've been had!" If anything, I wish
I was a better fighter, so I could join other fighters
To combat real terrorists, with their real weapons.

Peeping NSA

Monitoring dissidents, Occupiers and
Other outraged citizens, NSA goons
Get to hear dumb phone conversations
And dissect inane emails, but laptop
Cameras also allow them to watch
Folks stroking themselves as they
Log on to Porn Hub, while the NSA
Voyeurs also jerk off energetically
In their $3.2 billion headquarters.
(Unemployed perverts, do send
Your application to Fort Mead.)

Mass surveillance's main goal isn't safety
But intimidation and blackmail. Duh!
Which judges or congressmen are addicted
To call girls or child porn? Who rape teens?
Who have mistresses? Who hide in closets?
With mass surveillance, everyone is cowed.

Though they can't do anything without
Setting off a dozen red flags, they'll
Red flag you for writing in an email
Or merely googling: ""Plot,"
"Shoot," "torch," "attack," "Federal Reserve,"
"Car bomb," "dirty bomb," "cherry bomb," "da bomb,"
"Assassination" or "burn down Wall Street."
Though all they do is bomb,
They jump at the mere word.
Seeing and hearing all, they still managed

To miss that alleged Boston terrorist,
Though they have been warned repeatedly
By the Russians, "Hey, hey, dumbshits,
Watch that Chechen guy!" In truth,
They missed nothing. They knew exactly
Where Tarmelan was all along, up to
When they stripped and shot him, unarmed.

Then they got rid of two participating agents,
By tossing them from a helicopter, the way
Viet Congs used to be tossed. Remember
The SEALs who supposedly killed Bin Laden?
They too were killed by their own government.

There was no corpse, videos or photos
Of the world's most wanted man, only
A broken chopper tail, implying
A bungled raid, with casualties.
Sooner or later a SEAL would yak,
Refuting the official fairy tale,
So all these "heroes" had to be silenced.
Jerking media puppets, they laugh off
Each expose of their endless crimes.

As American soldiers raped Iraqi women,
They claimed Jessica Lynch had been raped,
Though she herself denied this, and
Though Pat Tillman was murdered
By an American sniper, they claimed
He was killed in a Taliban ambush.
For questioning their SEAL son's death,

A Philly couple was even molested by
The NSA's hairy palms and fists.

Since we can barely listen or remember,
They can lie to us without consequence.
For lying about doping, Barry Bonds
Was convicted of obstruction of justice,
But for lying about using the Bill of Rights
To wipe his mendacious ass, Alexander
Will probably receive the Presidential
Medal of Honor or Freedom, plus
Honorary Degrees from Brown and Yale.

The USA has become a one-way mirror,
And a one-way, high speed chase to hell.
In this perverted, capsized nation, the top
Criminals are lauded, while the selfless
And conscientious are caged, when not shot.

Hey, Homeland Security, FBI, CIA or NSA
Busy bodies following me as I'm typing this,
How low will you bend to scrutinize my nuts,
And is your petty power trip worth serving such
Sinister bosses, for they will turn on you, too?
Seeing and hunting so many enemies,
You will also be hunted and killed.

Zigzagging Forward

So forward looking, we see nothing
But a dystopian future, as in record
Breaking tornados, tsunamis, hurricanes,
Nuclear melt downs and a smiling Jesus.

All cops, firemen, teachers and garbage men
Are permanently furloughed. Toting uzis,
National Guardsmen and mercenary goons,
Native and foreign, patrol shopping malls,
Airports and stadia, which are reserved
For the beef, cake and chocolate eaters.

To hell with neighborhoods not behind walls
And guarded by a platoon. After dark,
Embittered riffraff lob shells into select
Zip codes, hoping to strike a CEO,
General or congressman. Though these sad
Rebels seldom hit anything, scores of them
Are routinely zapped by one of the millions
Unseen, hovering drones that don't just spit
Missiles and bullets, but also beam cheerful
Advertisements onto the sky 24/7: OPEN
HAPPINESS. I'M LOVING IT. There are also
Bug-sized drones for personalized attention.

What appears as a mosquito may actually be
A Pentagon drone, equipped with a single dose
Of FUCK YOU. Its tiny eyes can espy if you're
Disobeying one of the trillion no-nos, as posted
On government websites, though most folks

No longer have internet access, or even
A flushable toilet. The insect's software
Allows for various acts of summary justice,
From electric shock as a warning to prolonged,
Bedridden illness, to whimpering or screaming pain,
To an instant tete-a-tete with the long dead Bush.

The Pentagon has allowed that mistakes
Sometimes do occur, wiping out, in a flash,
Three generations or so, including vets
Of the Afghan, Iraq or China campaign,
But well, better be safe than terrorized
By shadowy terrorists. We're in a state
Of endless war, after all. Has been since 9/11,
Of what year, most Americans can't remember.

Education ain't what it used to be.
On every screen, boobs, pricks and puppies.
Remember when a high school senior could
Spell "corruption" or "surveillance"?
Remember when a college graduate
Could stab at the meaning of "torture"?
Remember when an intellectual wasn't
A droning muffler for serial outrages?

My babe's first words are "9/11," then "mama."
Draped in scavenged pillow cases, and armed
With bits of decaying wisdom, we zigzag.

To Flee Conjugation

Lugging my exploded home
And trampling on my own name,
I trek to a yearned deformation.

Imperial chaos hacks flesh,
Sends the unmeshed towards a
Capsized horizon. They dream
Of clean graphic design, houses
That don't collapse onto cribs.

Invaded, the invaded invade
The invaders' kitchens and,
Soon enough, bedrooms. Look,
They're invading each other.

Shut up, smug face, you know
Nothing of ugliness, even that
Which you've long bankrolled.

Tahseen Alkhateeb Interviews Linh Dinh

[First published in Arabic in Al Arab and Al Jadeed, both of London, in March of 2015]

Though you were born in Saigon, you spent most of your life in the US. Do you consider yourself as an American poet?

-Yes, very much so. A writer is defined by his language, above all, so anyone writing in English already belongs to that tradition of Skelton, Clare and Stevens. Although also important, subject matters come second. Though many of Isaac Bashevis Singer's stories take place in America, for example, he wrote exclusively in Yiddish, so he's seen as a Yiddish author. Yiddish was his mental universe. Having said all that, I can also claim to be a Vietnamese writer, since I also write poems, stories and essays in Vietnamese, and I speak Vietnamese daily. I'm two writers sharing one brain, which is probably a very dubious, if not catastrophic, proposition, but I would like to think it has actually helped me. Not entirely at home in any language, I can see how tenuous my claims to writing, thinking and even life is. I'm a very desperate person, frankly, but who isn't? Already an American poet by virtue of my shaky, shaking and shook up English, I'm also very much a part of this appalling socialscape because of what I write about. I've learnt how to become more of a hands on, down in the slush kind of writer. I get out there to see everything first hand,

and to hear people speak. I eavesdrop or strike up conversations, and sometimes barge into them, all in order to hear everyone's farcical, heart breaking or blood chilling anecdotes. I'm also out there to soak up their language, that is, their English, because this besieged yet cocky English is most fascinating. Also, for the last several years, I've become much more invested in writing that addresses issues that affect everyone, and that anyone can read, and since I live here in the United States, this reorientation has made me even more of an American writer.

How is it possible for you to freely separate between those "two writers sharing one brain"? How (and when) you decide to write "this" in Vietnamese and "that" in English? The "brain" decides, or the poem itself chooses its tongue, cadence, and transformations?

-I became reacquainted with the Vietnamese language by reading its literarure and translating it. While living in the US, I translated and published Vietnamese folk poetry and a book of new Vietnamese fiction. In 1999, I returned to live in Vietnam for two years and a half, and so I became very comfortable with Vietnamese, and yet, even then, I continued to write in English. It was during my time in Vietnam that I felt challenged to write in Vietnamese, but this did not happen until I left. In fact, I wrote and published my first Vietnamese poems while living in Italy, where I stayed for two years. As you well know, each language has its unique shades, hues, quirks, wickedness and sense of humor, and so a man who switches from one language to another becomes, essentially, a different actor. The Vietnamese language accentuates some of my emotional tendencies, but so does English. One language may be snarkier, starker, drier, more morose or abrupt than another, and syntaxes vary considerably, so a man who's familiar with at least two languages will inflect or contaminate each with the other. Since my Vietnamese writing shows American influences, both emotionally and linguistically, the reverse must be true also. Before I could write directly in Vietnamese, I merely translated my English language poems into Vietnamese. Later, though, some of my Vietnamese writing was so immersed in the language, it couldn't even be translated into English. The subject matters of some of these poems or essays would not be of much interest to an American audience anyway. For the last six years, however, I've been so preoccupied with my Postcards from the End of America project that I've written nothing in Vietnamese except for a poem and, for the occasion of Vietnamese New Year, three disquieting essays for a high-circulation Vietnamese-American journal.

You talked about your "re-acquaintance" with the Vietnamese language by reading, and translating, its literature. And also about the "return" or "the coming–back" to live again in Vietnam, when you "felt" yourself challenged to write in your own Mother tongue, but you couldn't write any, until

you left, and were living in Italy. Does that mean that you could find your own "Vietnamese literary voice" (if I may say) only in exile? (Especially when we read that your first book, *Fake House* (2000) was confiscated at Saigon's post office when you went to pick up an author's copy!) Does that "switching" point between the two languages you talked about (between their unique shades) needed you to be far away from the land where you were born, the land that "confiscated your first book," to achieve that "point of departure" from one tongue to another?

-My graduation into writing in Vietnamese was a gradual, natural process, and not subjected to any design. I returned to Vietnam to get away from the United States, then came back to the US to get away from Vietnam, only to end up in Italy, thanks to the intercession of my New York publisher. I do want to say something about writing from the outside. As an immigrant, I had to learn English from scratch, and to this day, I'm liable to make a basic mistake at any moment, but this precariousness is actually good, since it forces me to watch my step at each moment. As I've said to novelist Matthew Sharpe in an interview, "I'm a hyperconscious writer." That said, all writers are already hyperconscious, or at least much more paranoid about language than your average person. If you tussle with language at all, you know how tough, slippery and devious it is, and can make you look ridiculous at any moment. Further, any writer knows that language is an extremely malleable conceit, and its naturalness is merely a goofy illusion. Each word is bizarre, much less a bunch of them strung together, and it is often the native speaker who butchers his language worst of all, yet is quite gleeful and insolent about it. Commenting about one of my Postcards, a reader suggested that I should "ingrate" myself into more communities. Of course, he meant "ingratiate," but even that is wrong, for I'm just observing and talking to people, and not trying to kiss their asses for ulterior gains. Thinking of the wrong word, he confused it with another that's even more inappropriate. Of course, everyone makes linguistic mistakes nearly constantly, but since a writer is always dealing with language, he has many more chances to mess up.

With so many mind-scrambling gadgets, comprehension is more elusive than ever, but this doesn't prevent the sloppy reader and thinker from having vehement opinions on just about everything, and he's not shy about spewing his malaprop, off-the-cuff gibberish. If this was relatively rare, it could be laughingly dismissed, but one sees it everywhere now, so it has become a societal handicap, no less, and one that greatly assists the criminal elites in their husbandry of the bleating flock.

Getting back to the theme of writing from the outside, I published this in the *American Poetry Review* in 2004, "I've come to realize that I much prefer to live on the periphery of the English language, so that I can steer clear of the tyranny of its suffocating center. In this sense, I am a quintessential American. A Unapoet, I like to homestead just beyond the long reach of Washington [...] Hearing the rapid syllables of a foreign language, a bigot is infuriated because he's reduced to the status of an infant. Poets, on the other hand, should welcome all opportunities to become disoriented. To not know what's happening forces one to become more attentive and to fill in the blanks. Hence, poetry."

Please explain what you mean by Unapoet?

-Though highly educated, the Unabomber lived in a primitive shack in Montanta, away from mainstream society, so by calling myself a Unapoet, I was pointing out my existence away from mainstream America, which in that sentence is depicted as "the long reach of Washington." There is an American phrase, "the long arm of the law," meaning law enforcement can get you anywhere, and Washington, as "the world's police," can harass or even kill people worldwide. American culture also distorts one's perception, so by living outside of it (at the time), and away from its media and language, I could see the world (and America itself) more clearly. Though I'm back in the US now, I exist on the fringe and am connected to no institution. Like the Unabomber, I try to maintain my mental independence.

Though I don't send bombs to people, like the Unabomber, I understand his frustration with mainstream society.

Are you familiar with Arabic poetry and literature?

-I must admit to knowing next to nothing about Arabic literature. Nevertheless, I'll attempt a few observations about Mahmoud Darwish, since all writers can learn much from his life and work. First of, it is instructive and inspiring to see a poet who was deeply engaged politically, his entire life, without compromising his creative development. In fact, it was precisely his courageous willingness to grapple with the gravest crises affecting his community that gives his work such gravity. Though he tapped into timeless themes such as loss and homelessness, he never lapsed into a philosophical resignation, but struggled for justice, meaning and his people until the very end. He believed that words, and thus poetry, must matter. Though he didn't always write for the masses, he could reach them at will, and this achievement has become so rare that I can't think of a contemporary example. Although Darwish wrote many private poems that drew strictly from his personal life, he never forgot that poetry's most challenging and noble task was to give voice to an entire people. "A nation is as great as its ode," Darwish claimed most interestingly, because the implication is that a people's greatest canto, song or poem is its highest achievement, and not its pyramids, cathedrals, skyscrapers or aircraft carriers. Now, of course a poet will say that, you snicker, since it inflates his own status, but since words can survive even when bricks and stones have been pulverized, or when the country itself has been disfigured or dismantled, Darwish's assertion rings truer than ever.

In the early 20th century, when the French had already colonized Vietnam for 60-odd years, a Vietnamese intellectual, Pham Quynh, pronounced that as long as the nation's epic poem, Truyen Kieu, survives, the language and nation survive. This statement echoes, somewhat, Darwish's claim, but a people can't merely settle for a linguistic home. It can't feed and clothe its children or has a proper, dignified place in the world with just a song, no matter how great, so it's essential that the Palestinians, like the Vietnamese, regain their territory. Although there are ambiguities in Darwish's work, its overriding statement is abundantly clear, and that's Palestine has been stolen from the Palestinians by the Jews, to which he famously addressed:

"From you the sword–from us the blood
From you steel and fire–from us our flesh
From you yet another tank–from us stones
From you tear gas–from us rain

[...]

It is time for you to be gone
Live wherever you like, but do not live among us
It is time for you to be gone
Die wherever you like, but do not die among us
For we have work to do in our land"

In this entire poem, there is no bloodthirsty vengefulness, but merely a logical and quite restrained request for the invaders to get out!

As you have been lately involved in politics, how do look at the horrors done by the American Administration(s) to other nations: the invasion of Iraq and of Afghanistan, for instance? And what about their endless support for the Israelis despite their shameless war crimes against the Palestinians, whether in Gaza, or elsewhere?

-Oil and Israel are the two reasons for American criminality against the Muslim world. Without these factors, Muslims would not be so demonized and attacked by Americans, and this pattern will continue as long as Israel and oil remain. Israel is an unprecedented historical mistake, for it makes no sense to claim a right of return for Jews after 2,000 years, but deny the same to Palestinians after six decades, though many have lost their homes much more recently, for this landgrab is an ongoing process that won't end until all Palestinians disappear from "the Jewish homeland." It's tragic and farcical that a Chinese Jew can move to Jerusalem tomorrow, but not an exiled Palestinian who still has the key to his ancestral home. Israel is a violent concept that is executed and maintained with terror, and by this I mean American-sponsored Jewish terror, though these world class terrorists are so relentless with their propaganda, they have made "terrorist" nearly synonymous with their enemy, the Muslim. There is hope for Palestinians, however, for as the USA implodes, Israel will also go up in smoke. Working in tandem, the US and Israel have collapsed several Muslim governments and generated millions of refugees. The same fate awaits Israel, though its dissolution should be permanent, for only then will peace come.

Those living outside the US can't fathom the American media's extreme bias towards Israel. During the 2014 attack on Gaza, for example, American television viewers were only shown images of Palestinian buildings being blown up from afar, as if there were no people working or living in them. No corpses were seen being pulled from rubbles. While Palestinian victims stayed invisible, a single missing Israeli soldier had stories about him, with his portrait featured to emphasize his humanity. Unlike Palestinians, this Jew had a face. Female Israeli soldiers were shown sobbing over their fallen (male) comrades. When the massacre of Palestinians was finally over, there were articles about how quickly Gaza had gotten back to normal, so it was no big deal, you see, this butchering of 2,192 people (as compared to 77 deaths on the Israeli side). As if to prove this point, photos were shown of bustling Gaza streets, with kids happily playing.

On American television, there's a peculiar show called "Inside Israeli Basketball." Since the level of hoops in Israel is not particularly high, and its b-ballers are entirely unknown to an American audience, there is no sporting reason for this program, except that basketball is only a pretext to display Israel in a banal, and hence benign, light. Game footage and practice scenes make up only a small part of this show, for the camera often follows the players or coaches of Maccabi Haifa, the featured team, all over Israel. (Everywhere, of course, except Gaza and other troubled spots.) In one scene, one might visit a lovely beach, while in another, enter a Palestinian restaurant. Here, two teammates, an Israeli and a black American, enjoy camel rides, and one can see that they're very chummy with each other. The American, Ike Ofoegbu, gushes, "Here in Israel, the guys are very nice. They speak English, first of all, so they can interact with you. They're really friendly [...] To finally be here in Israel is very exciting. I'm just blessed to be here." Highly unusual for a reality show, there is no rancor or argument in "Inside Israeli Basketball," and no trashy behavior at all. Here, you won't find any screaming, backstabbing, jealousy or drunkenness, though these are the staples of just about every other reality show on American television. Always depicting Israel in an idyllic and harmonious light, this show is no more than propaganda, then, a carefully crafted mask to hide the endless violence needed to maintain this sham nation.

Though your poems were anthologized in Best American Poetry Series 2000, 2004 and 2007, and two of your prose poems were included in David Lehman's groundbreaking book *Great American*

***Prose Poems from Poe to the Present* (2003), and though *Village Voice* selected your short story collection, *Blood and Soap*, as one of the best books of 2004, BUT I sense, in one way or another, that your are still "away" of the mainstream literary scene. Is it so?**

-Yes, I'm only a tiny blip on the American literary scene, a barely noticed writer. My ten books of all types have gotten only a handful of reviews. A writer's only task, though, is to become a better writer, and since this is a lifelong, all-encompassing quest, it should leave him no time to worry about his career. Instead of schmoozing and networking with other writers, I've been getting drunk with plumbers, roofers, cashiers, jailbirds and cops, etc. If given a choice to spend an afternoon with a National Book Award winner or a manicurist, I'd choose the latter. Once a year, professional American poets attend a convention where they can suck up and screw down. Craig Santos Perez sums it up, "you get to travel to a fun city, you get to hear / meet many poets, editors, and publishers, you get to learn many things at panels, you get discount books, you get to eat at new restaurants, you get to dance, you get drunk, you get laid–what's not to like?" While that may sound terribly exciting to many poets, I'm not at all interested. Moreover, my politics, dozens of appearances on Iran's Press TV and opinions about Israel don't make me any more popular among my American peers, but, again, a writer should just concern himself with thinking, seeing and listening a whole lot better, and not fret about his professional standing. Instead of ingratiating, he should just hone his chops. I do care very much about making sense to everyone who's not a writer, however, and in this regard, I've made progress, for many ordinary people have sent money to support my Postcards from the End of America project. As a reader, I have to go way outside the mainstream to nourish my mind and spirit, so I don't mind being on the periphery as a writer.

Publisher's Weekly **(in its review of your poetry collection,** ***American Tatts*****) described you as "the rising star of the small-press world", and talked about your 'acrid ironies, [and] unmitigated disgust", saying that "Exploring disgust while toying with frames and assumptions, [you] become in one sense a real heir to Charles Bukowski." To what extent do you think that those "acrid ironies" and that "unmitigated disgust" make you a "real" heir to Bukowski?**

-I haven't read a whole lot of Bukowski and, frankly, don't see him as an inspiration. I do admire very much, though, his working class existence, and his deep sympathy for bottom dwellers of all kinds. He was comfortable around struggling people or outright losers, but along this line, American literature also has Jack London and William T. Vollmann, and Mark Twain also knew how to get down and dirty. The notion that literature wells up from the bottom, I also got from reading Vietnamese folk poems. Along with what's beautiful or transcendent, there's plenty that's foul, alarming or disgusting, so one must examine the whole gamut to have a balanced view of humanity and life. Cesar Vallejo urged, "doubt your feces for a moment," but the implication here is that shit often weighs on our minds. As a young man, I was also exposed to that crazy lineage of French writers which sprung from Rabelais and peaked with Artaud. From Louis-Ferdinand Celine, I learnt that a writer should never flinch.

You translated Eliot's "The Waste Land" into the Vietnamese, and the same work was also translated by the Vietnamese poet Nguyen Quoc Chanh. Why Eliot? And Why "The Waste Land"?

-When I was in Saigon in 2000, poet Nguyen Quoc Chanh asked me to look over his translation of "The Waste Land," and I made so many corrections, I figured I should do my own version. I didn't want to steal from Chanh, however, so I said that no line of mine would match his, and this is no easy task, considering there are 433 lines in that poem. Chanh ended up publishing his version in Vietnam, and mine appeared a little later in Vietnamese-American venues. Chanh is Vietnam's foremost contemporary poet, by the way, and he's the star of *The Deluge*, my anthology of new Vietnamese poetry. In any case, the decision to translate "The Waste Land" was made by Chanh because this major Modernist landmark wasn't available in Vietnamese. Readers are entirely indifferent to our two versions, however, and I can't say this surprises me. All the exotic cultural references make no sense to them, and I'm sure many are also annoyed by "The Waste Land"'s meandering and its footnotes. I've introduced a few American poets to the Vietnamse audience, but always only through a handful of representative poems. The first to translate Wallace Stevens, a personal favorite, I transposed "13 Ways of Looking at Blackbird" and a few others. Sometimes I translate a poem from an English translation, as in Nazim Hikmet's "On Living." I did Pablo Neruda's "Walking Around" while looking at both the original and different English translations. As you well know, the best poems are not always translated, and often it's simply because they're too challenging for a translator. A while back, I was asked about my opinions on translation, and below are some of my observations:

The best way to criticize an imperfect translator is to do a better translation.

Doing this, you'll make the imperfect, offensive translation, which you've sucked on and tweaked only slightly, disappear forever from the face of this earth.

The many resistances in the source poem force the translator to compensate and invent, enriching the language he is translating into.

In both cases, you have one culture or language trying to accommodate another. This meeting point, this border, this collision of avant-gardes, is where the new, improvised and unexpected can happen.

I'm not a translator so much as a tightrope walker between two unreliable dictionaries.

The worst translators are parasites and conmen, the best ones are parasites and pimps. I tend to think of myself as an honest and totally selfless charity worker.

Some of your short stories were published in anthologies and magazines as prose poems? First of all, do you believe in a "borderline" between prose and poetry? Then, is there any difference between prose poems and short stories? And, finally, what makes a "piece of writing" a good prose poem?

-There is definitely a border between prose and poetry, but the two forms do blend into each another. Most people think of a poem as having line breaks, and these dictate how a poem is read, but when there are no line breaks, can it still be a poem? Of course. Take Rimbaud's "Phrases," for example. Its absence of a narrative, ecstatic cadence and abrupt shifts within a sentence, and between sentences and paragraphs, all mark it as a poem. In fact, this is poetry at its purest:

"Should I have realized all your memories,--should I be the one who can bind you hand and foot,--I shall strangle you."

It takes a poet to come up with "realized all your memories," and to make the leap from "bind you," in a love poem, mind you, to "strangle you."

A similar passage might appear in the middle of a novel, and if it does, that's also poetry.

Conversely, many poems may have line breaks and rhymes, but contain only a minimal amount of poetry, if at all.

Though written in prose, Kafka's beautifully compact "The Wish to be a Red Indian" is also poetry. Since there's no story there, it can't be a short story.

Generally speaking, poetry is more tightly wound than prose, so you should get more protein with each bite. If this doesn't happen, you must promptly spit it out, demand a full refund (even if you didn't pay anything) and curse the fake poet, if not beat him up!

In your poems, you depict the "borderless body," not only as a naked existence where the "soul blossomed"—an existence that is open wide, "cleaned from all obsolete and labored presumptions"; the body "blends into all humans, animals and things" and "naked, walks through the street as the very first human," BUT also as an "erotic" existence that tends to free the body from its own "chamber music," from its own "language and meat," from its "obsolete maps": to overflow and seep into a "defiant puddle." Do you think that

one can never be a true poet without celebrating the "body electric"?

-This borderless body suggests the immigrant, a child in the womb, rapists, spouses, sitting in a bar and empathy. Human bodies are really one continuum that has been tragically yet mercifully broken up. If you're cut, I should feel pain, and vice versa, and when we're at our best, that's exactly what happens. Too often, though, people derive an orgasmic pleasure from watching another body being violated by a drone missile or a bomb. Excited, they cheer. Elias Canetti talks about how instinctively humans laugh at seeing somebody falling, and he traces this to our days as flesh hunters. Since a fallen body represents meat, we laugh out of joy. Beside this atavistic impulse, however, we also rush to help the fallen because we recognize the body in distress as our own. The American entertainment industry, though, is relentless in pushing the fantasy of the super predator, somebody who's capable of destroying countless bodies "of the bad guys." With its mesmerizing war and "action" films, Hollywood has amplified, to an insane degree, all of our worst sadistic tendencies. Sex, too, has become a matter of body count, but this is perfectly in line with the American obsession with numbers. As for your question about being a "true poet," there are so many types of poets out there, but I'd say the majority of them are not about grappling with the body's hidden logics, but smothering these with verbiage, for language, after all, is most often used to dissimulate and disguise everything, and not just the body. Having said that, neurotic poetry has its place, so a poet who always sidesteps the many bodies lying all around him, some smiling, some freshly killed, also has his place. Just days ago, a Vietnamese poet asked me to translate something, and so I did, "I'm aroused. I'm horny. I'm a whore. I'm an aroused whore. I'm an extremely horny whore." I'm not sure if she needed that for her FaceBook page, or if she was communicating directly to me, but it was clearly her body starting to speak. Not one to be rude, my body spoke back to her, but alas, only by email. Such is our postmodern world.

You spent the last seven years photographing the homeless, the angry, the "rebels" of America (or what I might call "the borderless bodies", borrowing the title of one of your books). Can you elaborate more on this "journey of the soul" (if I may say)? What things, in the first place, moved you to do such a thing: to document the other/ the real/the outrageous face of America? And to where, through those photos, you want us to go?

-Actually, it has only been six years. I started this photography project in 2009, when I got my first professional camera. At the time, I was making these art videos that incorporated poetry and still photography, but with my new camera, I started to roam the streets. Years before, I had been a housepainter so had known my city fairly well, but by 2009, I had become too alienated from it. I was staying home too much and sitting in front of the computer. It's telling that the last two major movements in American poetry, Flarf and Conceptual Poetry, are both media based and inspired. Like everybody else, many poets are enthralled by the internet. What you have, then, is language feeding on itself. Gleefully recycling its own waste, it stares at its flabby folds in the mirror.

Any important shift in society will show up in art, so if you have a blossoming bourgeoise, you'll see more middle-class images, and the advent of the newspaper, with its odd juxtapositions of serious news with ads, will usher in the collage. By the early 20th century, the newspaper had become a part of daily life in modern societies, so people were conditioned to seeing, say, a story about a murder or a rape next to an advertisement for shoes or candies. On a single page, you will see trajedies mingling with the ridiculous or trivia. These common yet jarring juxtapositions in low culture triggered similar strategies found in collage artists, surrealists, dadaists then, later, pop artists, etc. What's often lauded as radical art, then, is no more than an echo of a larger societal change, so it's really conformist in the extreme, and not radical at all. In a hyper mediated culture, the most radical act is to say no to all buffers and regain, touch by touch and one face-to-face conversation at a time, a more tactile reality, for it is, after all, your naked birthright.

Here, I'm talking about a resistence to media, not just its contents but its forms, and to clarify, I'll give you an example from my own life. In my late twenties, I decided to stop listening to recorded music. First of, it's highly unnatural and, I contend, even a sign of madness to subject oneself to endless noises that interfere with one's thinking and perception of the world. Music should be occasional, and by this I mean triggered by a very specific occasion, and not something kept on constantly to make its listeners deranged. Removed this buffer of recorded music and everything in the room becomes instantly more intense. Having said all this, I'd occasionally check out a song on, say, YouTube, just so I'd know what's happening in the culture. After reading about Miley Cyrus' supposed twerking, for example, I watched her performance on YouTube. Also, in my daily life, I can't help but hear recorded music, but when I'm at home, I function completely in silence.

With this conviction, I've walked out my door much more often, and just about everything I've seen contradicts what's broadcast relentlessly through the mainstream media, for daily, we're being told that the economic recovery is on course and unemployment is down, all positive news, but these are all lies, for if you'd walk down American streets and talk to ordinary Americans, you'd know how bad the situation is. Also, the parts of America that are most often seen by visitors are also extremely misleading, for Manhattan, Northwest Washington

DC or Miami Beach, etc., are but a glossed up façade to hide the rot that's spreading across this country.

For a while now, I have been aware of this nation's downward trajectory. In 2005, I taught a class called State of the Union. In it, I asked students to pay attention to their country's political, economic and social unraveling, and I challenged them to write politically relevant poetry. Though I've taught this writing workshop at various universities, I've pretty much stopped getting invitations to teach or even to read, and part of this is because of the deteriorating economy, but the bigger reason, I suspect, is because of my politics. You can't expect the academy to embrace you when you keep calling it a ponzi scheme!

Gouging students, American universities send young people to banks for loans that many can never repay, and it is the professors' job to hypnotize them into thinking they have a bright future. Saddled with terrible, sometimes suicidal debts, many will be stuck with low paying jobs that don't even require a college education, and even those with "practical" degrees will tumble into this abyss, for a collapsing American economy can't absorb its many college graduates. As if this isn't bad enough, foreign professional workers, as in engineers, doctors and nurses, etc., are also being imported to knock wages down. Though this is done deliberately to benefit employers, it's cloaked as a benevolent immigration policy so that anyone who questions it is accused of being a racist.

A huge pool of desperate graduates will also keep professors' wages down and render them dispensible, so what you have are all these docile and conformist intellectuals who are terrified of losing their jobs. The academy, then, is not a hotbed of debates but a padded playpen that delimits the terms of the discussion. There, only the more superficial or privately indulgent kinds of radicalism will be tolerated, for these don't upset the status quo or alarm the moneyed interests that are wrecking not just this country, but the entire world.

In sum, my project is a diary of America's ongoing collapse, and I've learnt much from roaming around. Before I started, I had never been to a tent city, for example, nor had I seen Los Angeles' Skid Row. Although Camden is only across the river from where I live, I didn't know it because, like most people, I had no reason to go there. With its absurdly high crime rates, it's also considered off-limits. Now, I have a much better understanding of Camden, as well as dozens of other cities I would not have visited. I've talked to hundreds of people I would not have approached.

It is ironic, though, that the internet provides me with a platform to report what I'm seeing and hearing. A rationale for this project is a rejection of media, of living life through a screen, but I'm only reaching you via a screen. For those living in the States, though, my images and words can only confirm what many are already experiencing, and if not, my project is an invitation to go out and see for yourself what's happening. For those outside the US, my project can be a window into an alternative America, one that's almost never seen. Mentally trapped in a virtual reality dished up daily by the mainstream media, even many Americans are not aware of how destitute or squalid huge swaths of their country have become. American poverty, though, is not the same as, say, the Vietnamese kind, and having lived in four different countries as an adult, and traveled to a few more, I do have some perspective on this.

America's relative affluence, though, is a direct result of her status as a super power. Running up the largest trade deficit ever, she is worse than broke, but mechandises continue to flow in thanks to the dollar's status as the world's reserve currency, but this arrangement is unsustainable. Soon enough, Americans will wake up to their true poverty, but in the meantime, the image that's still projected to the rest of the world is a USA that's obscenely rich, confident, fun and free of worries. As Harold Pinter said, "As a salesman [America] is out on its own and its most saleable commodity is self love. It's a winner," so there's a widening gap between the virtual America and the real one. When I posted a couple images of my own kitchen recently, a reader reponded:

"This might sound weird, but the photos of your kitchen are sort of reassuring. I live in the UK, and my kitchen is pretty much like yours, maybe a bit bigger but everything is from the 1970s and just staggering along. No dishwasher, etc. My US friends look aghast at me – 'no dishwasher? how do you survive?' And I think, 'What planet are you visiting from?' The advertising pics of America show huge kitchens, even the sitcoms of supposedly 'poor' people show incredible kitchens and meanwhile there's a hugely populated layer of people in the US (and the UK) that live on microwave meals or fast food because there's no place for them to cook anything. And then they get fat (and malnourished) from eating crap, and rich folks like my hedge-fund brother say 'look at that fat bastard, I'm not paying my taxes to support that.'"

The aim of my project, then, is to document the more hidden aspects of this country and also, through my political writing, to attempt to explain why it has become this way. Personally, this has resulted in my becoming more in touch with my city, country and time. I was tired of being in the poetry ghetto.

LINH DINH

Linh Dinh is the author of five previous books of poems, plus two collections of short stories, a novel and a non-fiction account of the economic, social an political unraveling of the USA, *Postcards from the End of America* (Seven Stories Press 2017). His political essays are regularly published at Unz Review and other webzines.

CHAX

Founded in 1984 in Tucson, Arizona, Chax has published 200 books in a variety of formats, including hand printed letterpress books and chapbooks, hybrid chapbooks, book arts editions, and trade paperback editions such as the book you are holding. In August 2014 Chax moved to Victoria, Texas, and is presently located in the University of Houston-Victoria Center for the Arts, which has generously supported the publication of *A Mere Ica*, which has also received support from many friends of the press. Chax is an independent 501(c)(3) organization which depends on support from various government and private funders, and, primarily, from individual donors and readers.

Recent and current books-in-progress include *The Complete Light Poems*, by Jackson Mac Low, *Life–list*, by Jessica Smith, *Andalusia*, by Susan Thackrey, *Diesel Hand*, by Nico Vassilakis, *Dark Ladies*, by Steve McCaffery, *What We Do*, by Michael Gottlieb, *Limerence & Lux*, by Saba Syed Razvi, *Short Course*, by Ted Greenwald and Charles Bernstein, *An Intermittent Music*, by Ted Pearson, *Arrive on Wave*, by Gil Ott, *Entangled Bank*, by James Sherry, *Autocinema*, by Gaspar Orozco, *The Letters of Carla, the letter b.*, by Benjamin Hollander, *Artifice in the Calm Damages*, by Andrew Levy, *Any Would Be If*, by Norman Fischer, *Leaves of Class*, by Kit Robinson, *A Night in the Sun*, by Will Alexander, and *Visible Instruments*, by Michael Kelleher.

You may find CHAX online at *http://chax.org*